ENGAGED COUPLES DEVOTIONAL

52 Scripture-Based Devotions
to Strengthen Your Relationship

TIFFANY NICOLE

ROCKRIDGE PRESS

Interior and Cover Designer: Stephanie Mautone
Art Producer: Hannah Dickerson
Editor: Mo Mozuch
Production Editor: Ruth Sakata Corley
Production Manager: Martin Worthington

Illustrations © Shelby Allison/Creative Market
Scripture quotations marked NIV are taken from the Holy Bible, New International Version®, NIV®. Copyright © 1973, 1978, 1984, 2011 by Biblica, Inc.™ Used by permission of Zondervan. All rights reserved worldwide. Zondervan.com. The "NIV" and "New International Version" are trademarks registered in the United States Patent and Trademark Office by Biblica, Inc.™

ISBN: Print 978-1-64876-857-6 | eBook 978-1-64876-858-3
R1

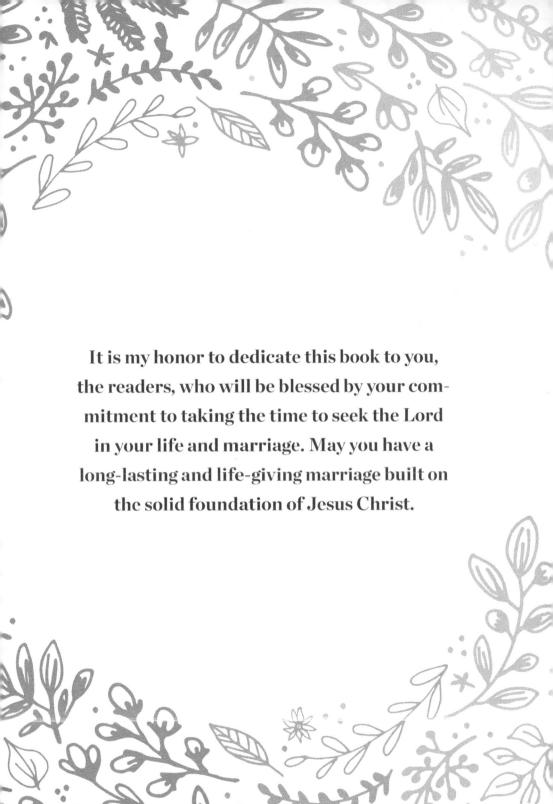

It is my honor to dedicate this book to you, the readers, who will be blessed by your commitment to taking the time to seek the Lord in your life and marriage. May you have a long-lasting and life-giving marriage built on the solid foundation of Jesus Christ.

Contents

Introduction

Congratulations on your engagement! This is one of the most exciting times of your life! I hope you're enjoying every single moment, but, real talk, you're probably learning that planning the perfect wedding is overwhelming. If you are anything like me, your "to-do" list is growing *exponentially*, and this makes it hard to stay focused on the other parts of your life that are just as important. Trust me when I say that preparing your heart for marriage is the best way for you to be spending your time as you prepare to say, "I do." During this season it is important for you to make space for the Lord and keep your eyes on Him. There will be a million things that demand your attention, but strengthening your relationship with God (and each other) should be your number one priority.

When you keep Jesus at the core of everything you do, you will see your marriage bloom and prosper. God wants to give you a loving and deeply satisfying marriage. Remember that the good fruit produced in your marriage is first cultivated from the good fruit produced through your relationship with Him. As you prepare to enter into the covenant of marriage with the person you love, you must not forget your first love, Jesus.

If you're reading this, odds are you want to create that happy, healthy, and long-lasting marriage with Jesus as the foundation. So, if that's what you are looking for, then you've come to the right place. The first year of marriage is often the hardest, which is why preparation is key. My goal is to equip you with the tools, resources, and conversations required for a successful marriage *ahead of time*, so that when the enemy attempts to come between you and your happily ever after, your marriage will be like a strong fortress that cannot be shaken.

I know because my own marriage went through the gauntlet of trials and testing. When I got engaged, I interviewed married couples young and old, asking for their best advice on marriage. I was terrified of divorce and borderline obsessed with ensuring my marriage stayed the course of blessings and prosperity. The only problem was, I wasn't really following the Lord, and neither was my future husband. Despite all my best efforts to ensure marital bliss with my own strength, my marriage did not last. That is why, first and foremost, keeping Jesus at the center of your relationship is *crucial* to a successful marriage.

Despite our best efforts in doing things the right way from a secular perspective, we didn't do the one thing that truly mattered, which was seeking Christ first. The truth is, if even one of you isn't following the Lord, it won't matter how much premarital advice you seek, your marriage will be unbalanced and not rooted in the solid foundation of Jesus Christ. Jesus tells us that when we read His word and obey His commands, we are like a wise man who builds his house on solid rock (Matthew 7:24). I want your marriage to be built on the solid rock of Jesus Christ, which is why my goal in this devotional is to prepare you for a marriage with Christ at the foundation. As we walk through each week's Bible verse and lesson, I want to encourage you to be open and vulnerable with each other. Is it uncomfortable? Yes, but it is totally necessary. The more honest you are with each other, the more prepared you will be to enter into one of the most precious seasons of life, marriage.

How to Use This Book

We're going to closely examine every aspect of marriage *before you enter into it*, so you know exactly what to expect. Each week you will read the Bible verse and the devotion that goes along with it, which illustrates and explains the major takeaway from the verse. Then, at the end of every devotion, there will be an activity for you to do that's designed to prompt further discussion or action that you can take into your daily life. Throughout this devotional we will discuss major marital topics like the true meaning of marriage, love, forgiveness, faith, finances, and family planning, to name a few. Each devotion is designed to help you open up and be honest with your partner so that the two of you can flush out some of these topics now, before your wedding, instead of during your marriage. I also want to encourage you to pick a day each week to read through that week's devotion and activity. This way you've already carved out time from your schedules when the two of you can sit down and prepare for your future marriage together.

Making the Time

I don't have to tell you that divorce runs rampant these days. I mean, it's not exactly news to say it's become quite normal.

It has been estimated that one-half of all marriages will end in divorce. With projections like these, should the idea of a lifetime commitment to a partner even be viewed as a realistic expectation?

In a July 2000 article in the *Washington Post*, author and philanthropist Philip D. Harvey even goes so far as to say, "A reasonable level of divorce may be a symptom of a healthy and mobile society." Although some divorces are necessary, to say that divorce is *healthy* for society is a bit much. However, can you honestly blame people for doubting the future of a lifelong marriage when you see projected statistics like a 50 percent divorce rate?

Don't despair, your marriage is not doomed. However, the trials of marriage will come no matter your level of faith. Being a Christian doesn't guarantee a good marriage, and not being a Christian doesn't guarantee a bad one. However, what I can tell you with 100 percent certainty is that marriage is God's idea. The Bible actually *opens* with a marriage when God brings Adam and Eve together in holy matrimony. It also *ends* with a marriage when Jesus brings His bride, the church, to Himself in the wedding feast of the lamb.

Even though marriage is God's idea, you need to know that long-lasting, life-giving, and unconditionally loving marriages don't just happen. Not even in the Christian world. They are the deliberate result of two determined people who are willing to make it work with God's grace and strength. So, do you have time for this devotional? Honestly, probably not. But I challenge you to *make the time*. The future of your marriage could rely on it.

Marriage Is God's Idea

So the man gave names to all the livestock, the birds in the sky and all the wild animals. But for Adam no suitable helper was found.

Genesis 2:20 (NIV)

T his verse is profound because it shows that, from the very beginning, marriage was God's idea and His design. In Genesis 1, aka creation week, the Bible tells the story of when God creates, well, *everything*. As God creates the waters and the ground, the sun and the moon, and the animals both on the land and in the sea, He sees everything that He has created and declares it "good." Then God decides to make human beings in His image, to be like Him (Genesis 1:27). Upon looking at everything He has made, He reflects upon His work and says it is "very good."

Genesis 2 is actually a retelling of creation week, but it focuses on the creation of human beings. After He creates all of the other things in heaven and on earth, God immediately gives them His stamp of approval by declaring them "good." However, with the beginning of mankind we see something different. Here we learn that God actually doesn't create man and woman at the same time but creates the man, Adam, first. However, Adam is somehow incomplete. The first time in the Bible God tells us that something is "not good" is in reference to Adam being alone. How interesting.

In Genesis 2:18, God promises to make Adam a "helper" who is exactly right for him, so that he does not have to be alone. Before Adam even desires to have someone to share his life with, God sees his singleness and declares it not good. So, God goes about making Adam a helper with whom he can enjoy the divine covenant of marriage.

You see, we were created for fellowship with God, but we're also created to have fellowship with others. Marriage is intended to fulfill our need to love others and receive love from others. Marriage is, and has always been, God's idea, not man's invention.

This means marriage is not something we should enter into lightly. It's important to understand the true significance that God always intended marriage to have. God doesn't want you to be alone; God wants you to have a happy, healthy, and long-lasting marriage full of excitement, tenderness, intimacy, and love.

However, regardless of how much you love each other, everyone is flawed. We will still bring sin and brokenness into marriage. Everyone marries a sinful person; there is no "perfect" marriage free of sin. However, because marriage is God's idea, God understands it. This is why following God's principles allows your marriage to not only survive the hardships that come with every marriage but actually thrive—thrive for you, thrive for your family, and ultimately thrive for the Kingdom of God.

> ***Exploring the Scripture:*** *Just as God did not want Adam to be alone, God doesn't want you to be alone. There are numerous places in the Bible where God tells us He is with us and will never abandon us. Read Bible verses Isaiah 41:10 and Romans 8:38-39 and discuss how these relate to this week's devotion.*

Marriage Is God's Gift

For this cause shall a man leave his father and mother, and shall be joined unto his wife, and they two shall be one flesh.

EPHESIANS 5:31 (KJV)

G od always plans to meet the needs of His children, even our emotional and physical needs. Before Adam is even aware that something is missing in his life, God knows exactly what Adam needs. God is more aware of our every need than we can possibly imagine. He alone knows the inner workings of our hearts, and He alone knows what's truly good for us.

What God sees (even before Adam) is that earthly companionship is *good* for us. It's good for our hearts and meets our emotional, physical, and spiritual needs. Actually, marriage not only meets our needs, but it goes *above and beyond* in meeting our needs. Marriage is God's gift to us. It's a gift for us to experience the excitement of finding someone special; we then board the roller coaster of emotions that comes with sharing and expressing those feelings of love and intimacy.

Countless books, movies, poems, and songs have been written about the mystery and romance of love. It's impossible to escape or ignore. A common phrase for someone who's found love is "you've caught the love bug." This phrase is ironic, because it sounds almost as if love is something that you want to avoid. But no matter how hard you try, you are simply no match for its power. When we are in love, at least at first, it's a whirlwind of emotions that consumes our hearts and minds. As Mr. Darcy says in the 2005 *Pride and Prejudice* movie adaptation, "You have bewitched me, body and soul." Love makes you feel like anything is possible, like life is all of a sudden worth it.

In 1 Corinthians 13, the author speaks of love being the greatest thing we could possibly give or be given in return. In it we read beautiful descriptions of love: how it never gives up, never loses hope, keeps the faith, and holds on no matter what the situation. Then the author, Paul the Apostle, concludes the chapter with one of the most profound statements in the Bible on love: that when everything is said and done, only three things will last forever—faith, hope, and love—and the *greatest* of these is love (1 Corinthians 13:13) (see "Love Is the Greatest," page 118).

So, although Adam already had the love of the Father in the Garden of Eden, he didn't have Eve. God gave Eve to Adam as a *gift*. Your partner is also God's gift, one that is not to be regifted or exchanged. A lifetime partnership through marriage is the best gift that God could give, and you should love and honor each other accordingly.

> ***Reflection Questions:*** *Why do you think God gave you the gift of your partner? What did you need? In what ways does your partner support your physical and emotional needs? How do you support theirs? How can you show your partner you are thankful for their role in your life? Think deeper than gifts and greeting cards.*

Marriage Is a Depiction of the Image of God

So God created man in His own image, in the image of God created He him; male and female created He them.

GENESIS 1:27 (KJV)

You could probably describe marriage in a lot of different ways: a loving relationship, unity between two partners, complete trust and devotion, a lifelong commitment, and on and on. But I bet you would never have thought to describe marriage as a depiction of the image of God. However, when God originally created Adam and Eve, the Bible says He created mankind in His own image, which includes both men and women.

You see, in the Old Testament, when God creates Adam, the original Hebrew word used for man is *ha'adam*. *Ha'adam* doesn't mean "man" exactly; it really refers to mankind, humanity, or "the human being." So, we really shouldn't even look at God's first human being as "Adam" at first, but simply as a human being created in the image of God.

However, in the part of the story when God creates woman from the rib of the man, the word "rib" also tends to be mistranslated. The Hebrew word used is *tsela*, which is used 40 times throughout the Old Testament and translated every other time as "side" or "half." So what we really see happening in the human creation story is God creating woman from "half" of man. God originally creates one human being made in the image of God, but upon creating him God declares, "It is not good for the man to be alone." So, God splits the human being apart, creating two separate beings made in the image of God (see "Marriage Is God's Idea," page 1).

This distinction is also shown in the original Hebrew. The Hebrew word *ha'adam* is used when referring to the original human being, but after the creation of man and woman, the Hebrew words *ish* for "man" and *ishshah* for "woman" are used.

Now, what's also interesting is that God is neither male nor female. He's actually described throughout the Bible as *both genders*. The Bible describes God as a being with masculine characteristics, namely His description as God the Father (1 Corinthians 8:6), and at other times with feminine characteristics, such as His comparison to a laboring woman (Isaiah 42:14). This is because the person of God encompasses *both the masculine and the feminine,* because that is the nature of *who God is*. That means the image of God also encompasses these traits. The masculine alone or the feminine alone cannot be an accurate representation of the full image of God. Instead, the full image of God is represented *the best* by the unity and oneness of both halves coming together in holy matrimony. Man and woman represent complementary halves of the one original human being that God created.

This also explains why God cares so deeply about marriage—it is a demonstration of His image upon the earth. Marriage is a representation of God's good work, the completion of both sides of God coming together to form the full image of God. It's as if, when two people unite as one through their commitment of a marriage covenant, God stamps their unity with the seal of His image.

> ***Exploring the Scripture:*** *What does it mean to be made in God's image? It's a pretty cool concept, but one that can be difficult to wrap your head around. Read Genesis 1:26-27 and 2 Corinthians 4:4. Write down what you find regarding what it means to be made in the image of God.*

Marriage Is a Covenant

For this cause shall a man leave father and mother, and shall cleave to his wife: and they twain shall be one flesh.

MATTHEW 19:5 (KJV)

A lot of people argue that the institution of marriage just isn't practical anymore. You'll hear people depreciating the value of marriage by saying things like "Marriage is just a ceremony," or "It's just a piece of paper."

However, when a couple prepares to get married, they need to understand what they are doing. Their decision to be joined together through marriage actually invites God into the equation, because marriage is God's idea. God Himself is the one who joins the couple together. To God marriage is not just a ceremony or a piece of paper, it's a *sacred union*.

Your relationship might have started out as a simple commitment to each other, but the moment you decide to get married God raises it up to a higher level—a *covenant*. But what is a covenant?

A covenant is an agreement between two or more parties to perform certain actions. You'll find throughout the Bible that God makes all kinds of covenants. You've got the Old Covenant, the Mosaic Covenant, the Abrahamic Covenant, the Davidic Covenant, and the New Covenant, just to name a few.

God actually raises marriage up so that it is not just an agreement between two people but an actual covenant by which the spouses pledge themselves to each other in all aspects of their lives "until death do us part." It's not a contract to be honored or broken; it's a covenant that will last forever.

In the book of Malachi, we see how marriage is held up *as a covenant* made before God. Malachi 2:14 says, "The LORD is the witness between you and the wife of your youth. You have been unfaithful to her, though she is your partner, the wife of your *marriage covenant*" (NIV) (italics added).

We see the same concept in Matthew 19:5–6 when Jesus links the romantic relationship between spouses with a *divine covenant.* In Matthew 19:5 we see the romantic relationship between partners. Two people have fallen in love and decided to come together.

However, Matthew 19:6 continues and says, "So they are no longer two, but one flesh. Therefore *what God has joined together*, let no one separate" (NIV) (italics added). Here we see the divine covenant part. What was once only a human experience, a commitment and relationship between *two people*, Jesus now says is a covenant between two spouses *and* God.

Marriage vows are a verbal expression of the lifelong commitment to each other made in your mind and in your heart. It's the richest fulfillment of the promise of eternal love and commitment that we can experience with another human being in this life. When we speak the vow "from this day forward," we mean a lifetime. That's God's design. This promise is not meant to be broken. Your marriage covenant is a sacred union between you, your partner, and God that should be protected and cherished. It's a promise of faithfulness, trust, security, and love, now and forever.

> **Prayer:** *Lord, help me see my future marriage the way you see it. Help me view it as not just a marriage but a marriage covenant, a sacred union between my partner, me, and you, as we cherish our love for each other and commit to each other the same way you love and are committed to us.*

Bone of My Bone, Flesh of My Flesh!

And Adam said, This is now bone of my bones, and flesh of my flesh: she shall be called Woman, because she was taken out of Man.

Genesis 2:23 (KJV)

D on't you just love Adam's response when he first sees Eve? Okay, maybe you don't now, but trust me, you will. When God brings Eve to Adam he exclaims, "At last! This is now bone of my bones and flesh of my flesh!" That probably doesn't sound super flattering to all the women out there, but trust me, this is ancient Hebrew for bow-chica-wow-wow. It's as if Adam is saying, "Finally, God! You've brought me a hottie." Actually, it's even better than that.

When reading this verse, we have to keep in mind that God has just brought all of the animals to Adam so they can be named; however, none of them is a good companion for Adam. When Adam finally sees Eve, he is ecstatic to have someone who is *just like him* (see "Marriage Is God's Idea," page 1). It's way beyond the fact that Eve has the same physical bones as him or that her flesh resembles his; Eve is made in the same *likeness* as him. She is human, just like Adam, and there is an immediate connection between them that is different from what Adam could ever have with the animals. Eve fits Adam perfectly.

In verse 23, we see Adam actually getting a bit poetic, as many people who are in love do. The verse "This is now bone of my bones, and flesh of my flesh: she shall be called Woman, because she was taken out of Man" is actually written in a poetic fashion. Fun fact: Verse 23 is the first poem, or, more precisely, the first poetic couplet, in the Bible. Take a look at this verse in your own Bible at home. Most Bibles show the poetic nature of this verse by stacking up and separating these lines from the rest of the text to show that they're different from the rest of the narrative.

Scholars have even noted that the poem has a rhythm to it. The first line has a two-beat rhythm, and the second has a three-beat rhythm. This is fascinating, because it's as if, when Adam first sees Eve, he is moved to speak in verse. Essentially, Adam sees the woman God has brought to him, and all of a sudden, he's breaking out into song and dance for her! And is it any surprise mankind's first song is a love song?

Now, it might seem like "bone of my bone and flesh of my flesh" aren't the most romantic words to sing over your beloved, but there's actually a reason this feels a bit lackluster to us. It's actually hard to translate and convey the emotion of the original Hebrew, an emotion that is missing from the English translation.

However, a very loose translation of what Adam says when God brings Eve to him would be "Wow, now this is it. This is the one that will complete me!" Adam gets emotional and actually sings to Eve with joy because God has brought him his perfect match. Someone who is just like him, a mirror image of himself, and yet different.

> ***Weekly Opportunity:*** *Don't hate me for this, but what I want each of you to do this week is write a poem, rap, or song (it doesn't have to be long) expressing your love for your partner. If you really want to get into it and come up with a dance—hey, I'm all for it. Now, if the idea of this is daunting, don't get too bogged down with making it rhyme or getting it perfect. Just write what's in your heart and how your partner makes you feel. When you are finished, share what you wrote with each other.*

Leave and Cleave

---

*For this cause shall a man leave his father
and mother, and cleave to his wife.*

Mark 10:7 (KJV)

When a couple is joined by marriage, the Bible makes it clear that they must leave their mother and father and "cleave," or join together, with their partner. When I first read this, I thought it sounded like such antiquated advice. I mean, I moved out of my parents' house when I was 18, but I didn't get married until I was 26. And I wasn't a solo case; that also seemed to be the trend for a lot of my friends. For that reason, I used to feel this verse made no sense in our modern world. However, I was wrong—very, very wrong. This verse is actually very practical for couples today.

Even though most people don't live at home with their parents until they are married, the mindset shift that this verse speaks about applies 100 percent. You see, marriage requires severing one relationship to solidify another relationship. Maybe you don't need to leave the nest physically, because you've already moved out, but you might need to leave the nest emotionally, financially, and even spiritually.

You will need to cut the cord of dependence on mom and dad to create a new first loyalty to your future spouse. This doesn't mean you abandon your mother and father, but it does mean you need to establish an adult relationship with your parents that gives space to you and your partner to truly be united as one.

This is huge, because some couples never leave their parents *emotionally*. Or sometimes your marriage can be held hostage because your parents won't detach from *you* on an emotional level. You see, your parents will never stop being your parents. They love you and will always feel like they need to "parent" you no matter how old you get, which is why the idea of "leaving" can actually be more traumatic for parents than for children. Your parents' role and function in your life are shifting, and that can be hard to accept. But it's absolutely crucial that you make the mental, emotional, and spiritual shift from depending on your parents for all of those needs to instead depending on each other.

Now, the word "cleave" is interesting, isn't it? Most translations use the word "join"; however, that word just doesn't quite express the true meaning of the original Greek word used in this verse. "To cleave" means "to adhere to, stick to, or join with." Think of cleaving as being joined together so closely and unitedly that it's as if you've been glued together. It is a unique joining of two people into one entity or, as the Bible says, one flesh (see "Two Become One Flesh," page 23). There is a permanence associated with that word. Cleaving means not giving up when things get tough and always being willing to work things out. It means loving each other, praying for each other, forgiving each other, and having an open heart to admit when you are in the wrong.

Failing to "leave and cleave" creates a lack of intimacy and, potentially, a breakdown of your marriage. That is why leaving and cleaving is the foundation to building the strong and sturdy marriage God desires you to have.

> ***Reflection Questions:*** *In what ways do you anticipate you will struggle with leaving and cleaving? Are there areas of dependency that are hard to let go of? Will it be harder for your parents than it is for you? Why? What can you say to them to make it easier?*

Compatible,
yet Different

And the LORD God said, It is not good that the man should be alone; I will make him an help meet for him.

GENESIS 2:18 (KJV)

In Genesis 2:18, the one thing that is declared "not good" in all of God's creation is Adam being alone: "And the LORD God said, 'It is not good that the man should be alone.'" The same verse also includes God's *solution* to Adam's loneliness: He will make Adam a helper who is a perfect fit for him. Marriage is ultimately a depiction of the image of God. This was not a mistake! It was part of God's brilliant design (see "Marriage Is God's Idea," page 1).

This tells us that Adam was somehow insufficient on his own, and Eve was God's solution to Adam's deficiency.

The word "helper" is the Hebrew term *ezer*. What's interesting is that *ezer* is used frequently throughout scripture when referring to God as *our* helper (Psalm 70:5, Psalm 33:20). Does this mean that God is somehow subservient to humans? Definitely not! It means that God actually comes alongside us and *partners* with us to support and strengthen us when we are weak. It's a gift and a blessing to have God as our helper; it's not a term that should indicate a role of inferiority.

In the same way, the creation of Eve as Adam's "helper" indicates that she is the perfect gift that corresponds to Adam's exact need, and he to her need. The two are created to complement each other. They're compatible, yet different. She is meant to support and strengthen him, and he to support and strengthen her. But their roles for going about this are different. Adam and Eve are equal to each other, but their roles in each other's lives are different.

As you prepare to walk into marriage, it's important to understand that your partner is equal to you, yet your role in each other's lives is different.

Eve is created to be Adam's complement, the perfect counterpart to himself—one formed *from him*, a perfect resemblance of himself, to complete what is lacking in him. In other words, she is created to be his person. A match specifically for him. She's not greater than Adam, nor lesser than, but she is equal to him—the person God has chosen to be at his side doing life with him.

Your future spouse is also the person who has been chosen to be your complement, the perfect counterpart to yourself. In the dating world we frequently say, "Opposites attract." It's interesting that the Hebrew word *kenegdo*, which is typically translated into English as "suitable," literally translates as "the opposite to."

So, when the Bible refers to Eve as Adam's "suitable helper," it could be equally as accurate to think of Eve as Adam's "opposite helper." She's Adam's missing link. She fills up the missing pieces in Adam that he is lacking, making him whole.

> ***Reflection Questions:*** *What are a few ways your partner is compatible with you, yet very different? Describe how your partner's opposite qualities complement you. For example, are you extroverted, but your partner is introverted? Are you messy, but your partner clean and tidy? Are you detail-oriented, whereas your partner is better at seeing the bigger picture? Are you more methodical and structured, but your partner is more relaxed and carefree? How are your partner's differences from you a gift and benefit to your life?*

Two Become One Flesh

And they twain shall be one flesh: so then they are no more twain, but one flesh.

MARK 10:8 (KJV)

O *oh là là*, and then the two became one flesh. It's hard to ignore the very important physical and sexual aspect of the "one flesh" that the Bible is referring to. However, this union is infinitely more than just physical. There is an emotional, psychological, financial, and spiritual bonding that happens between two people in a marriage. In fact, it's a bonding of *every aspect of life*. It's a uniting of two people who are intended to be so tightly knit together that it's as if these two people have become *one person*.

Now, when the Bible talks about one flesh, it really means one flesh. God's design for marriage is for two people to truly become *partners*. It is a joining together of two different yet compatible people who are intentionally made for each other by God.

What's interesting is that the Bible says the two will *become* one flesh. This means you and your partner will not instantaneously be one flesh on your wedding day. Instead, it's a process that takes time. It doesn't happen automatically upon taking vows. It grows and develops as you deepen your relationship with your partner and begin to trust them more and more.

Sharing your life with someone is not simple, even when it's the person you want by your side forever. You can love your partner deeply, but there are likely still areas of your life you've put a fence around, topped with barbed wire, and a warning sign saying, "Off limits."

Maybe you know *exactly* what area of life this is for you. Maybe you don't. However, if the idea of tearing down that barbed-wire fence absolutely terrifies you, I want to assure you that this is the fun part. It shouldn't frighten you but excite you. It's *fun* to continuously discover new things about your partner. I distinctly remember a time when, after seven years of being with my husband, I looked at him, shocked, and said, "Wow, I never knew that about you!" There are *layers* to people, and unraveling those layers piece by piece is part of the process of becoming one flesh.

The human heart desires to be fully known and fully loved, and that is what one flesh is all about. It's to be fully known by your partner, flaws and all, and still be fully loved. But getting to that point is not an overnight, instantaneous, snap-of-the-fingers kind of achievement. It's a lifelong process.

That is why the process of becoming one flesh is commonly referred to as "weaving." Think of your marriage as a union held together by threads, which are woven together over time. Every day, week, month, and year your marriage is being woven together into one flesh, making it immovable and strong.

> **Prayer:** *Lord, we pray for the walls in our relationship to be torn down. We desire a marriage that is open and vulnerable and a safe space where we can become the one flesh that your word declares. Help us open our hearts to each other so that we can be both fully known and fully loved.*

Naked and Unashamed

And they were both naked, the man and his wife, and were not ashamed.

GENESIS 2:25 (KJV)

The Bible can be a bit risqué, and this verse is no exception. I've always found it interesting that God's original design for Adam and Eve was one of nakedness. Naked here means to be bare before, and with, another person. There's something absolutely beautiful about standing before your partner completely naked and not being embarrassed or ashamed about it. It conveys a certain level of intimacy between you and your partner that you have chosen to share only with them.

As discussed elsewhere in this book, cleaving joins a couple together so closely that it is as if you have become one flesh (see "Two Become One Flesh," page 23). Part of becoming one flesh is developing a deeper level of *intimacy* in your marriage. There's this moment when all of your walls have been torn down, and you are literally standing before another person naked, completely exposed. Exposed physically but also exposed emotionally, open and unashamed before another person.

That is why intimacy is way more than sex. Intimacy is the deep and rewarding connection between two people, physically, spiritually, emotionally, and socially. Deep down everyone longs for intimacy, even though not everyone is comfortable pursuing it. The goal for an intimate marriage with your partner is to be both loved and fully known by them.

If you're loved but not really known, you may feel comforted; however, your relationship lacks the emotional depth that the Lord wants the two of you to experience. To be fully known and still truly loved is to be loved as God loves us. It's what we need to liberate us so we can stop pretending. It fortifies us so we can face any difficulty in life. That's what godly marriage brings to us, to be fully known and still fully loved.

In fact, marriage is meant to be the most miraculous and tender form of intimacy that you could ever experience with another human being. To be completely known by another person, and to still be loved and accepted by them. To transparently share your life with someone else, whether it be your joys, hopes, sorrows, dreams, disappointments, or achievements.

For many of you it might be a lot easier for you to be physically naked before another person than it is to be emotionally naked. And that is okay, because becoming "one flesh" takes time (see "Two Become One Flesh," page 23). But just know that the oneness of marital sexual intimacy is only possible when the oneness of emotional intimacy is first established, because "one flesh" doesn't begin with your body, it begins with your heart.

In fact, true intimacy is *only possible* when there is a deep relational unity between you and your partner. This is because the reality of sexual intimacy and emotional intimacy are extremely intertwined and were never meant to be separated. Modern societies often separate the two, but this was never part of God's design. So, if you desire to have a rewarding and intimate sex life, it begins with having a deep and intimate emotional life where your marriage is a safe haven of mutual love and respect.

> ***Reflection Questions:*** *What are some ways you can open yourselves up to each other emotionally? What areas of your life do you feel are "off limits"? Write down a few areas of your life that come to mind immediately, and I challenge you to pray over what you have written down. Ask God to help you open your heart to your partner so you can be more vulnerable in all areas of your life.*

Sin Destroys Intimacy

Then the eyes of both of them were opened, and they realized they were naked; so they sewed fig leaves together and made coverings for themselves.

Genesis 3:7 (NIV)

Marriage is infinitely rewarding at its best and indescribably miserable at its worst. So I'm going to be very frank about this—the *number one thing* that will prevent you from having a deep and intimate relationship with your partner is sin. *Sin destroys intimacy.* When you have intimacy, marriage is rewarding, but when you don't, it's miserable.

We see this in the Bible. God tells Adam he can freely eat the fruit of every tree in the Garden of Eden except one—the tree of the knowledge of good and evil. If he eats of its fruit, he will surely die. However, in the next chapter of the book of Genesis, temptation sets in as Adam and Eve disobey the Lord. They eat the forbidden fruit, and their disobedience leads to sin and death entering the world; however, what's interesting is that the Bible doesn't explicitly state this. In fact, all we're told is that both Adam's and Eve's eyes are opened, and they know that they are naked, so they sew fig leaves together and cover themselves.

We've discussed elsewhere that Adam and Eve's nakedness is symbolic of the love, trust, and intimacy shared in a marriage. But now we're seeing all this break down *as a repercussion and consequence* of sin. Suddenly, Adam and Eve aren't comfortable being naked and exposed anymore, whereas before, they weren't even aware of their nakedness. Furthermore, out of fear of being naked and exposed, Adam and Eve cover themselves up with clothing, trying to *hide* their nakedness.

This is the world we live in. We all "cover" ourselves up by building walls and defense mechanisms around the things we are most uncomfortable with. However, the point of intimacy is to tear down those walls as you establish love and security with your partner.

Every single one of you will enter into your marriage wearing "fig leaves" that cover up the things you don't want anyone, including your partner, to see. But as the two of you become one flesh, this "clothing" will begin to come off, restoring your marriage back to God's original design where you're both standing before each other naked, without shame.

And because it is sin that causes Adam and Eve to put on clothing in the first place, guess what will cause you to put your "clothing" back on, even after intimacy is established? That's right, sin. The obvious solution is to simply not sin against each other, which is a thousand percent easier to say than do. Most people don't intentionally hurt the person they love, yet it still happens. This is why we must be aware of the division sin causes. We must acknowledge our weaknesses so that, when we enter into marriage, we will cherish the love and trust we've worked so hard to build.

Reflection Questions: Think of a few ways you know you have a tendency to sin against your partner. Maybe you know that you're not the most patient person, and it hurts your partner when you react harshly out of frustration. Maybe you know that you tend to put your work above your relationship, which causes your partner to not feel loved. Write down a few areas of your life that you know are weaknesses, and then share your list with your partner so you both can be more mindful of them in the future.

Love Covers a Multitude of Sins

Above all, love each other deeply, because love covers over a multitude of sins.

1 Peter 4:8 (NIV)

If you thought I was going to tell you sin destroys intimacy without also telling you how to *restore* intimacy, think again. The purpose of this book is to prepare you for a long and happy marriage, and restoring intimacy is a key to getting you there. So, if sin is the *number one thing* that prevents you from having a deep and intimate relationship with your partner, what's the number one thing that can restore intimacy? You guessed it! Love and forgiveness.

Let's look at our relationship with God. It was the repercussions of Adam and Eve's *sin* that destroyed the intimacy between us and the Father. What happened that allowed us to be restored to the Father once again? In a word, Jesus. But in a few words, love and forgiveness.

It was Jesus's great act of selfless love for us that paved the way for our sins to be forgiven and for us to be restored to an intimate relationship with God. Jesus has shown us that love and forgiveness are the yellow brick road to relational restoration. Remember, Peter tells us that love *covers* a multitude of sins.

There's that "covering" again. Are we noticing a pattern yet? When God originally designs Adam and Eve's marriage, they are automatically "covered" by the love and presence of God, allowing them the freedom to be naked and unashamed, completely open and intimate with each other. However, when sin enters the world, Adam and Eve's relationship with God changes, because sin separates us from God. Their sin results in them being banished from the Garden of Eden, *the very presence of God*, causing them to lose their "covering."

Without the covering of the Lord, they feel ashamed at their nakedness, causing them to cover themselves artificially with fig leaves so they will no longer feel exposed. This "covering" not only breaks the intimate relationship they share with the Lord, but it also breaks the intimate relationship they shared with each other. But that's not the end of the story. In 1 Peter the author tells us that it is *love that actually covers our sin*. And not just one sin, but a multitude of sins.

In the same way that Jesus's great love for us covers our sins, it is our great love for each other that covers our partner's sins. No one is perfect, and we all fall short of God's holy standard, which is why we must continually show love to each other even when we don't want to. This isn't easy. It's extremely hard to forgive someone when we've been hurt. But the longer you hold onto those feelings of hurt and anger, the deeper the wedge you will drive between you and your partner.

This is why it's crucial to lean on the Lord to help you forgive. Jesus is the ultimate example of love and forgiveness, especially for people *who do not deserve forgiveness*. We need to lean on His strength to show us how to love, because when we choose to love and forgive each other despite our mistakes, that is when relational intimacy is restored.

> *Exploring the Scripture: To "cover" sin is to forgive sin, and forgiveness is directly associated with love. The best example of a love that covers sin is Jesus's sacrifice on the cross. Read Ephesians 2:4-5. What do these verses teach you about love, forgiveness, and grace? What do they reveal to you about how you and your partner should handle love and forgiveness?*

Marriage Is a Mystery

This is a great mystery: but I speak concerning Christ and the church.

Ephesians 5:32 (KJV)

I f you've ever read Ephesians 5 before, you know that it is a *dense* chapter, but man-oh-man is it good when properly understood. Right before Paul says, "This is a great mystery: but I speak concerning Christ and the church," he quotes Genesis 2:24. Genesis 2:24 says, "That is why a man leaves his father and mother and is united to his wife, and they become one flesh" (NIV) (see "Leave and Cleave," page 17). We cover this verse elsewhere in this devotional, but it's crucial to understand that this verse is *key* to understanding God's purpose for marriage. We know this because it gets quoted repeatedly throughout the New Testament. Jesus quoted this verse in the Gospels when teaching on marriage, and now we see the Apostle Paul quoting it in Ephesians 5 when teaching on marriage.

Pro tip: When God repeats Himself throughout scripture, He is trying to tell you something important, and you should pay attention.

So, the repetition of Genesis 2:24 tells us that having a thorough understanding of this verse is *extremely significant* to understanding what God is saying about marriage in general.

What does Paul tell us about Genesis 2:24? That it's a great mystery! The reason it's a mystery is that the meaning of marriage goes way beyond the actual covenant being made. The meaning of marriage is ultimately an illustration of *your relationship with Jesus.*

Here's the thing: Paul doesn't use the analogy of marriage as a way to describe Jesus and the church; it's the other way around. God designed marriage as a way to explain the coming of Jesus for His bride. Now, here's what gets me excited about this. At the time of Genesis 2:24, *there was no Jesus Christ in human flesh yet.* And of course, there was no church in need of cleansing and saving yet, either.

Paul wants us to understand that marriage isn't used to clarify the coming of Jesus; the coming of Jesus was used at the very beginning of creation to give meaning to marriage. When Paul says, "This is a great mystery: but I speak concerning Christ and the church," he is saying that when Christ came into the world and died for the church, He did so to cleanse her and present her to Himself in splendor *as His spouse.* Even though at the time of Genesis 2:24 there was no incarnate Jesus Christ, and there was no bride, aka the church.

Before the beginning of time and the foundation of the world, God knew His plan of salvation through Jesus Christ. He knew He was going to unite Jesus with the church just like He unites us in marriage. In Ephesians 5, Paul is using Genesis 2:24 to explain that our entire understanding of marriage is based on the sacrificial love found between Christ and His church.

Yet that was the meaning of marriage from the very beginning. God already knew He was going to unite Jesus with the church before Adam and Eve ever sinned, which is why He created marriage to represent the covenant love between Jesus and the church (see "Marriage Is God's Gift," page 4).

Reflection Questions: In what ways do you also see a correlation between the love found within a marriage and the love between Jesus and the church? Be honest here. If the correlation seems farfetched, that's okay, too. Ask God to reveal to you how His design of marriage is the perfect reflection of the love between His Son and the church.

Submit Yourselves to Christ

Submit yourselves therefore to God.

James 4:7 (KJV)

In order for the biblical roles of marriage to be carried out properly, one thing first and foremost needs to be true: Both partners in a marriage must be submitted to Christ. The English Baptist preacher Charles Spurgeon says, "A man is not far from the gates of heaven when he is fully submissive to the Lord's will." The fact that we call Jesus "Lord" implies that believers are submitted to Jesus's will, but it's still worth asking ourselves how submissive we really are. I know many born-again believers who love Jesus and fully believe in Him yet still struggle with submitting themselves to His will. In fact, I could have included myself in that category until only a few years ago. I wish I could say I always knew that God's way was best and never strayed from His perfect will for my life, but, alas, that isn't my story. Like a stubborn horse, I blazed my own trail for years and only reconsidered my course of action once I'd messed my life up a bit. By that point, surrendering to Jesus was easy. I practically threw my hands up in the air and said, "Jesus, take the wheel! You couldn't possibly mess things up more than me."

And, honestly, that's how a lot of people finally submit to Jesus. Submission is rarely our first choice; it's often a decision we come to when nothing else has worked. But when you realize that submitting to Jesus's will for your life doesn't harm you but actually makes you flourish, you'll find it *easy* to submit to Him. You begin to realize that even though other people might let you down, Jesus never will. Even though other people might not have your best interests at heart, Jesus always does. You come to a point where you realize that there is nothing to fear in a life fully surrendered to Christ, because Jesus's plans for your life are *always* better than yours.

You might be wondering, "Well, what does submitting to Jesus look like? How do I know whether I'm doing it correctly?" Easy. Simply put, submitting to Jesus looks like obedience to Jesus. It's humbly coming to the feet of Jesus and asking Him to transform your heart into the image of Christ. It's recognizing that Jesus's ways are better than your ways, and willfully *choosing* to live a life in full surrender to the will of God. Proverbs 3:5 says, "Trust in the LORD with all your heart and lean not on your own understanding" (NIV). Submitting yourself to Christ is choosing to believe that it's okay if everything doesn't make logical sense to you, because you're not leaning on your own understanding; *you're leaning on His.*

And when it comes to marriage, that's exactly what Jesus is asking you to do. God doesn't want you to lean on your own understanding of what makes a marriage work; He wants you to lean on *His understanding.* God wants you to apply what the word of God says regarding marriage and live a life in full obedience to Him, even if you don't completely agree with it. As believers, we have to trust that the God who created marriage knows more about it than we do, and because we trust in Him, we can also trust in what He says about marriage.

> ***Exploring the Scripture:*** *Read Psalm 9:10, Proverbs 3:6, and Psalm 37:5-6. What do these verses have in common? What does God promise for those who trust in Him?*

More Than a Feeling

My little children, let us not love in word,
neither in tongue; but in deed and in truth.

1 John 3:18 (KJV)

C an I be honest with you? One of the main reasons I came to Christ was because I was on a journey to understand love. Funny sequence of events, right? Here I am trying to understand the meaning of love, and then bam, I have an encounter with Jesus that changes my life forever. So, I know you must be wondering, how exactly did this happen?

Well, at the start of my journey I had just broken up with a boyfriend I genuinely loved with all my heart. We began our relationship with all of the feel-good emotions you would expect: the euphoria, the butterflies, the fireworks, and the blissful feeling that you and your beloved are the only two people who exist in the world. Early on in our relationship, I couldn't imagine us fighting, because it was just so easy to love him.

Plot twist: Three years and two broken hearts later, we decided to call it quits after months of what felt like *nonstop fighting*. How could a relationship that started off with such strong feelings of love and devotion have possibly gone so wrong? I thought I knew what love was, but I ultimately realized I had no clue. I felt lost and confused.

So, acting as a true millennial, I turned to Google for answers, which, through a series of testimonials on the love of God, finally led me down the path of salvation through Jesus Christ. Through Christ, I realized that love is so much deeper than a feeling, because, ultimately, it's an action. The "feeling" of love that we experience in the early stages of dating is easy to celebrate, but what do you do when that feeling fades? Is your love over? Did it die, never to be seen again?

No, your love didn't die; it just changed its shape. There will be a point in every relationship when that euphoric feeling fades, but that doesn't mean your actual love for your partner has faded. Most of us tend to focus on the "falling in love" part and use these feelings of love to determine the duration of the relationship. But let's be real, falling in love is easy to do. In fact, it's effortless. But guess what? Falling out of love is easy, too. The true challenge is keeping love alive, because that takes work.

It's a choice you both must make, because staying in love takes real commitment. Before the two of you take vows, you must understand that at some point, the rosy glow of your relationship will wear off. When that happens, you have a decision to make. Are you truly committed to loving this person forever? Or are you harboring an exit strategy in the back of your mind for the day you might want to let them go? My prayer for you is that you understand that love is more than a feeling—it is a commitment to show love even if you don't feel like it. I know this sounds hard, but when you demonstrate the *action* of love even when you don't have the *feeling* of love, you will experience what it means to truly love like Christ loves us, which is the greatest gift you could ever give someone or receive in return.

> ***Weekly Opportunity:*** *Make a list with your partner of all of the reasons you love each other. Write down as many as you can think of. Write down the serious things that pull at your heartstrings and are full of emotion. Write down the silly things that no one else gets, and only you and your partner would understand. Even write down the small things that just make your life a little easier. Keep this list in a safe place and read it to each other when you find yourselves drifting apart or at a challenging point in your marriage. Use it as a constant reminder of the "loving feeling" you share.*

Value Your Partner above Yourself

Do nothing out of selfish ambition or vain conceit.
Rather, in humility value others above yourselves.

<small>PHILIPPIANS 2:3 (NIV)</small>

Philippians 2:3 is one of those verses that sounds amazing on paper but in reality is very, *very hard*. The general idea here is that we are to value others more than we value ourselves. This goes back to the fundamental principle that the first and second greatest commandments in the Bible are to love God and love others (Matthew 22:37-39). Nowhere in the Bible does God tell us that the path to true happiness is putting ourselves first above others and valuing our own happiness as our number one priority. Instead, the tone found in the Bible is starkly different; it emphasizes the importance of humbling yourself and serving others above yourself. The idea of loving yourself isn't even a concept found in the Bible!—which is dramatically different from the "love yourself" mantra we hear from the world.

So, what are we to make of this? Does God not care about your emotional well-being and happiness? Should your entire life be one of self-sacrificial martyrdom? Well, yes and no. As you go about fulfilling the first commandment of putting God first and leaning on the love of God to fill you up spiritually and emotionally, He will then begin to reveal to you your true identity in Christ, which, sidenote, is a real confidence booster. The Bible says you are loved, seen, worthy, fully known, and fearfully and wonderfully made. And that's just the beginning. But it is with this renewed sense of self-worth that the second commandment of loving others becomes almost second nature. In fact, it becomes your *heart's desire* to do what felt nearly impossible before, serving others and putting their needs above your own. This is the way the overflow of God's love operates. You are so full of God's love that when it comes to loving the people around you, *it becomes easy*. However, your future spouse is not just another person within your friend group; for all intents and purposes, your spouse has now become an extension of *yourself*.

How's that the case? Well, when you get married, who you are apart from your spouse *no longer exists*. There's only you and your spouse now. You are now one unit, one body, and one flesh, and as you enter into marriage, becoming one with your spouse is now your new identity. So, if you come home looking out for your own interests and view your spouse as someone whose sole purpose in life is to make you happy, then ultimately you are *not* going to be happy, because no one can fill those needs, not even your spouse. But if your perspective is that God has put you in this relationship to serve your spouse and make *them happy*, and your spouse's approach is to serve you and make *you happy*, then you are both mutually serving each other, and *you will both be happy* (see "You Lose Your Life to Find It," page 147). Your joy comes from serving your spouse, their joy comes from serving you, and at the end of the day, this serves everyone—including God.

> ***Weekly Opportunity:*** *What are some ways you can put your partner first? Make a list in private and try doing some of them throughout the week. Take an inventory of your partner's response. Did it help your relationship or make it worse? How can you incorporate some of these things into your everyday life?*

Prevention Prayers

For the eyes of the LORD are over the righteous,
And His ears are open unto their prayers.

1 PETER 3:12 (KJV)

P rayer is powerful. It's like an invisible force that enables God to move on our behalf and create real transformation and change in our lives. In fact, God promises us that when we cry out to Him and call upon the name of Jesus, He hears our prayers and will respond. However, many people think this is only necessary when something really terrible has happened, or when you need God to get you out of some sort of bind. That's definitely not the case. Some of the most powerful prayers you can pray are prevention prayers. These are prayers of blessing over your relationship, your children, your family, your career, your church, even your relationship with God.

In 1 Peter 3:12 we read that the eyes of the Lord are on the righteous, and His ears are open to their prayers. I always found this confusing, because I never thought of myself as "righteous." So, let's first address the "the eyes of the Lord are on the righteous" part. Did you know that if you are a believer in Jesus Christ, then your faith has made you righteous before God (Romans 3:22)? This was definitely news to me. I would read verses like this one and think, "That's why my prayers aren't getting answers; I'm not a righteous person!" However, just because I didn't *feel* "righteous" doesn't mean that I'm not righteous in God's eyes. Once I understood that by my faith I have been *made righteous*, I realized that this verse and many more are for me to use and apply to my life.

It's because we have been made righteous before God that God hears our prayers and His ears are open to our needs. This means we can pray for anything and everything, and as long as it is in accordance with God's will, it will be done. So, I suggest that the two of you, as two people preparing to enter into marriage, take this to heart and start praying over your future life together. Even if everything is sunshine and roses right now, it's still important to pray a prayer of blessing and unity over your life.

So, what do prevention prayers look like? Well, they actually look a lot like giving thanks. You can thank God for all kinds of things, like blessing your marriage, prospering your finances, or shining His face upon your wedding day. However, the real power in prevention prayers is that they establish a system where you both come to God with an issue before, or as, it arises in your life. This way, when something does happen, you are both already in the habit of asking God to intervene—before a potential problem becomes serious enough to cause division.

This is the beauty in having a forever partner who can stand with you through every season of life. You can depend on each other to lift each other up in prayer, believing for the things of God. What a gift! At some point there will be things that will begin to come between you two, but instead of letting these things divide you, use prevention prayer to come together in holy unity and pray the blessings of God over your marriage, your life, and your future together.

> **Prayer:** *Heavenly Father, we thank you so much for bringing the two of us together in marriage. We pray that our union glorifies you, and our lives are filled with love for you and for each other. Thank you for giving us the tools and resources to prepare for marriage and for blessing our future life together.*

Till Death Do Us Part

*What therefore God hath joined
together, let not man put asunder.*

Mark 10:9 (KJV)

D oes this verse sound a bit intense? It does to me. The idea of spending the rest of your life with the same person can be intimidating; however, I think the intensity of this verse is 100 percent intentional. I would contend that the way modern society tends to view marriage actually *lacks* a certain level of intensity. You see, marriage was *always* designed to be a lifetime commitment. In God's model of marriage, there is no calling it quits. But society has made divorce easy; one of the most common reasons for divorce these days is "irreconcilable differences," which honestly can mean whatever the heck you want it to mean.

Throughout the course of a marriage, it's completely valid and real to begin to think things like "I don't feel valued anymore" or "I don't value them anymore." Or to begin wondering how a marriage that started off so great could turn into what feels like nonstop arguing. It's important to note that there is no perfect marriage, and it's precisely when you go through tough times that you'll find God wants you to fight for your marriage and not give up on what He has brought together.

Someone once said that marriage is like flies on a screen door. Those that are in want to be out, and those that are out want to be in. The grass is always greener. Other people may seem to be in a better situation than you, but in reality, they probably aren't. That other person who seems appealing will have just as many flaws as the person you're with. Things just *look* better from the other side. It boils down to simple human nature; it's hard to be completely satisfied with where we are in life all the time.

But that's exactly why we need to work through the rough spots; this is where true obedience to God comes into play. When the Bible says that no one should separate what God has joined together, it quite literally means that you've made a vow to be with your partner until death. The two of you have become united as one flesh, and as one flesh you operate as an inseparable unit despite the hardships that come between you.

According to Harvard-trained social researcher and author Shaunti Feldhahn, the average first-marriage divorce rate is around 20 to 25 percent. Perhaps you've heard the claim that Christians are just as likely to divorce as non-Christians, but that's not entirely accurate. The claim has been attributed to a 2004 study by the Barna Research Group; however, when examined further, the numbers were based on survey-takers who identified as culturally "Christian" but didn't necessarily live a *committed Christian lifestyle*. In reality, Feldhahn found that those who are active in their faith and church community actually have a 25 to 50 percent *lower* divorce rate than non-churchgoers.

This is good news! People who keep God at the center of their marriages and family tend to stay married at far greater rates. And not only stay together but thrive! How can this be? Well, one of the main reasons for this is that they submit their lives to Jesus, not their partner (see "Submit Yourselves to Christ," page 40). This means depending on Jesus as your source of patience, kindness, goodness, faithfulness, and love so you can turn around and love your partner the same way Christ loves you.

> ***Reflection Questions:*** *How has the prominence of divorce in modern society affected your outlook on marriage? Have you had to overcome any fears in regard to committing to your partner? Does knowing that there are lower divorce rates in marriages where both parties live a life committed to Christ ease your mind about making this commitment?*

Good Stewards

As every man hath received the gift, even so minister the same one to another, as good stewards of the manifold grace of God.

1 PETER 4:10 (KJV)

Surviving the "for richer, for poorer" part of your wedding vows begins with understanding that God has a plan for your finances. We have to come to the realization that, first and foremost, everything belongs to God. The earth and everything in it is God's, thus everything we have has been given to us by God. The Bible makes it clear that God is the one who enables us with the ability to make money (Deuteronomy 8:18). In 1 Corinthians 4:7 Paul even asks how we can possibly boast about anything, since everything we've been given is from God.

So, as you prepare for marriage, it's helpful to acknowledge that everything you have comes from God. In fact, the Bible repeatedly calls us "stewards," which means someone who looks after or manages someone else's wealth or property. It's important to note that stewardship is not just a part of the Christian life, stewardship *is* the Christian life. Everything we do revolves around stewarding the gifts that God has given us. You can even argue that marriage is stewardship because God has entrusted you with His son or daughter to love and care for, for the rest of your life. That, in and of itself, is stewardship.

When it comes to being a good steward of your finances, you want to agree together on how to use the money that God has given you. It's one thing to agree on how you will use your money; it's an entirely different thing to agree to use it in a way that is pleasing to the Lord. So, how does God want you to be using your money? Well, we have to remember that God's purpose in marriage is for two people to become one flesh. We all think of the "one flesh" part of a marriage as primarily physical and emotional, but I would contend that it's even financial, meaning *how we use our money.*

Coming together in a godly marriage involves sharing everything you have with your spouse, including your money, which is why you would be hard pressed to find a Christian marriage counselor recommending you keep your money separated. The reason is that you don't want to leave a financial backdoor open for your own secret spending. Through marriage you want to be united in all things, including your finances.

The goal is to no longer view your finances as "my partner's money" or "my money" but instead think of it as *"our money,"* with the understanding that ultimately everything you have is *God's money.* As believers we must understand that it is not our own abilities that allow us to create wealth, but it is God who supplies us with the ability to make wealth. The money that we have been given may be a little, or it may be a lot, but regardless of the amount, God calls us to honor Him with our wealth by being good stewards of what He has given us.

> ***Exploring the Scripture:*** *Read Psalm 89:11, Psalm 24:1, and Haggai 2:8. How does reading these verses change the way you view your money and finances? How does it make you feel to know that everything you have is actually God's? How do you feel about combining finances as a married couple? What possible conflicts do you see occurring? How can you resolve them?*

Commanded to Love? Wait, What?!

A new commandment I give unto you,
That ye love one another; as I have loved
you, that ye also love one another.

John 13:34 (KJV)

T he Bible tells us on multiple occasions that we are *commanded* to love. We read it in John 13:34, but let's also look at 1 John 3:23, "And this is his command: to believe in the name of his Son, Jesus Christ, and to love one another as he commanded us" (NIV). As Christians, we are called to love one another, not because we *feel* love for them but because we are *commanded to love them*. The Bible teaches us that love is a *determination of the will* that comes out of obedience to God, who *commands* us to love.

Now, does this sound cold to anyone else? Okay, God, you're *commanding* me to love? Come on! Where's the romance? Excuse me if I'm not overflowing with warm fuzzies.

So, let's address this head-on. On the surface, it 100 percent seems like loving each other out of pure obedience to the Lord is an inferior kind of love to the butterflies and fireworks we typically associate with the love feeling. And make no mistake, I am right there with you. (One of my favorite movies is *Sleepless in Seattle*, if that gives you an idea of where I stand on the spectrum of hopeless romantics.) But I have learned from personal experience that loving each other out of commandment and action is *far more loving* than loving each other because of a feeling.

Why do I say this? Well, we may start off thinking that "love" can only look a certain type of way. But there is something to be said about the kind of love that is shown when you absolutely do not deserve it—when you have been beyond cruel to the person you love the most and you've said the very thing that you know can tear your partner down in an instant. A marriage relationship is supposed to be one of openness and vulnerability, but there's a real danger and risk in that. When you open yourself up emotionally to another person, you're giving them keys to your heart that can either lift you up or tear you down. Sometimes, your partner will choose the latter out of pure anger and spite.

So how then is the commandment to love *greater* than the feeling of love? Well, it's because someone is *deciding* to love you, even when you don't *deserve* to be loved. That is true love. It's easy to love someone you are absolutely smitten with. What's hard to do is love someone you can barely look at, or even think about, because they've cut you in those deep, hidden places that only someone close to you could touch. This is when "love" does *not* come naturally. It's simply not natural to love someone who frankly does not deserve your love. Yet this is the type of love Jesus commands us to show to our partners. This love chooses to continue loving them, whether they deserve it or not.

Reflection Questions: In what ways does being commanded to love seem inferior to the feeling of love? In what ways is the commandment to love superior to the feeling of love? Tell each other a story of a time when you chose to be loving toward someone else (whether it be a parent, child, friend, or foe) out of obedience to the Lord. What were the results of your obedience?

First Fruits

Honor the LORD with your wealth, with the firstfruits of all your crops; then your barns will be filled to overflowing, and your vats will brim over with new wine.

<small>PROVERBS 3:9-10 (NIV)</small>

When it comes to managing our money, and really, our lives, the whole idea behind the Christian walk is that everything belongs to God, and we are stewards of the resources God has given us. The key principle behind this is that God owns everything and we simply manage *His money* (see "Good Stewards," page 56). This is a concept that so many of us struggle to understand, myself included. I grew up thinking that everything I earned was *my money*. I might as well have put it away in a vault with giant red tape around it saying, "Danger! Electric shock hazard. Do not touch." Just the thought of giving away my precious, hard-earned money practically gave me shortness of breath and mild hives. At the risk of sounding completely stingy, I even got annoyed when friends got married or pregnant because my first thought was, "Crap, now I have to spend all this money to get them a present, book a hotel, buy a dress, etc." I know, I know. Either you're silently judging me and sarcastically thinking, "Wow, what a *great* friend you are," or it's quite possible that *you can relate.*

Either way, I wasn't exactly embodying the characteristics of a fantastic friend, because I was too self-absorbed, thinking only of how my money could best serve yours truly. I can imagine that it's because of these Scrooge-like qualities that the Lord has done a number on me precisely in this area, asking me to tithe and give away more money than I was comfortable with for years. However, as I gave away more money, a funny thing began to happen: Money's hold on my heart began to loosen its grip. The girl who never parted from her precious pennies has now been transformed into a "cheerful giver" (2 Corinthians 9:7) who tithes way more than she could ever have imagined. And loving it, might I add! Well, for the most part—I've come a long way, but I'm still no St. Teresa. And that's fine, because giving away everything you own isn't the point. God's way of giving has less to do with the actual money being given (although that's also important) and everything to do with the generosity and obedience of your heart.

When Proverbs 3:9-10 speaks of honoring the Lord with your wealth and the firstfruits of your crops, this means God is asking you to give part of your income to Him *first*, before you do anything else with it like pay bills or go shopping. Heartbreaking, right? However, that's why we have to understand that it's not like our tithe is *God's money,* and the rest is *our money. All of it is God's money.* Every single dollar bill belongs to God, and we are mere *stewards* of what is, and always has been, *His.* As stewards of God's money, we are responsible for, and will ultimately be judged by, how we *manage* His money. However, this should give you hope, because Jesus tells us that when we are faithful with the little we have been given, God knows we can be faithful with much more. And it is because of our faithfulness and obedience that, as Proverbs 3:10 says, we will be blessed for our obedience to the tithe.

> **Prayer:** *Lord, help us understand that everything we own is ultimately yours. Show us how to best spend our money so that it pleases you. Help us become united in our finances so that we can use them for the glory of God.*

Love Your Enemies

But I say unto you, Love your enemies, bless them that curse you, do good to them that hate you, and pray for them which despitefully use you, and persecute you.

MATTHEW 5:44 (KJV)

D oes this verse sound odd to anyone else? If you've been following the Lord for any amount of time, you will know that this
verse is one of many that represent how the wisdom found
in the Kingdom of God is completely different from the wisdom found
in the world. Oftentimes Jesus tells us to do the exact opposite of what
we typically *want* to do. He tells us to love our enemies, bless those who
curse us, do good to those who hate us, and pray for those who spite-
fully use us.

Enemies, curses, hate, someone who uses me? Yes, Jesus, please sign
me up. All of those things sound exactly like the kind of person I want
to love . . . NOT! Let's be real, how can this be the way the Kingdom of
Heaven is run, when the world that I live in runs *completely* differently?
Yet, despite what seems "right" or "fair" in our own heads, this is exactly
what Jesus is asking us to do. We are commanded to love our enemy,
especially when our "enemy" is the person lying on the other side of the
bed. Which brings up the giant elephant in the room: There may come a
point when your partner, *the person you love the most in this world,* will
suddenly become your greatest enemy.

What will you do then? Seek vengeance? Tear them down? File for
divorce? Well, according to the Bible you should do none of those things.
What *are* you supposed to do? Love them, bless them, and pray for them.
Sound simple enough? Maybe, maybe not. That's why I want to walk you
through exactly how this looks in real life. When we choose to love someone because we are commanded to love, and not because they *deserve* to
be loved, something very powerful happens. God meets us exactly where
we are, in ways we can scarcely understand.

Imagine this scenario: Your partner has hurt you deeply, and now
you're giving them the cold shoulder. You haven't spoken in days, and
your relationship is starting to look like something from a Wild West
cowboy shoot-out. You're both silently circling each other with intensity
as a tumbleweed blows past, your hands on the holster in anticipation.
If they have the nerve to say even one more thing, then you're ready. It's
just a matter of who's going to draw first. Secretly, you're exhausted by
the whole debacle, but you'll go to the grave before you cave first.

But then you remember Jesus's commandment to love your enemies. You think, "But God, I don't love them right now." God says, "I know that, because I can see your heart, but what I want you to do is love them anyway." You protest, "But God, you don't understand! I don't *have love* for this person." God says, "I know that, too. But what I'm asking you to do is to step out in obedience and *act lovingly* toward this person, even if you don't *feel* love for them." That is exactly where the supernatural meets the natural. The moment you *step out* in obedience to the Lord is when the Lord *steps into* your situation and works in ways you couldn't possibly begin to understand.

> **Prayer:** *Lord Jesus, I acknowledge that your ways are higher than my ways, and your thoughts are higher than my thoughts. Some days it feels like I do not understand you at all, yet I choose to continue to trust you. When you say that loving my enemies is good for me, I believe you. Help me walk in your ways and in obedience to you.*

True Love Is Sacrificial

---

*And walk in love, as Christ also hath loved us,
and hath given himself for us an offering and a
sacrifice to God for a sweetsmelling savour.*

EPHESIANS 5:2 (KJV)

Ephesians 5 opens with the two most challenging things you will ever be asked by God to do: 1) show love even when you don't feel like it, and 2) sacrifice something you value in order to show the love that you don't even feel. How are we supposed to do this? Paul gives us clues in the letter to the Ephesians, telling us that in order to be able to walk this out, we need to be imitators of God. To imitate means to follow as a model or to copy a person's speech or mannerisms. If we are to imitate Jesus in the area of love, then we are to love others the *same way* Jesus loved us.

How did Jesus love us? Well, He gave up His life for us. Jesus sacrificed His own life in order to give us life, demonstrating what true love actually is through this noble act. Jesus shows us that sacrificial love is the greatest form of love that you can possibly express.

Sacrifice is the act of giving up something you value for the sake of something or someone else. This is key, because if you give up something that you don't value, it's really not much of a sacrifice, is it? If it's easy to give up, then it probably never meant that much to you. But when you give up something that *is* difficult to let go of, you enter into the uncomfortable realm of *true sacrifice*.

Ephesians 5:2 is telling us that we are called to love each other the exact same way Jesus loved us, which is a love that is sacrificial. Easy, right? Wrong.

Let's put this together: First, we're told to love our partners even if we don't *feel* love for them, which is extremely difficult in and of itself. Second, we're told to give up something we value greatly in order to *show* that person our love. Who else feels like this is mission impossible, especially if your love for this person is fading fast?

Honestly, it's easy to give up the things that we care about when we adore someone. I remember in the early stages of my marriage both of us were more than willing to bend over backward for the other. It was easy to agree and compromise, even on large life changes like leaving our first real home and moving across the country or deciding to get a pet.

But the true testing of your marriage will come when you are asked to show sacrificial love for your partner even when times are tough, and it isn't the easiest to love them. Or when what you are called to sacrifice for the relationship is truly painful. Imagine having to work two jobs so your partner can go back to school, or opening your home to your spouse's parents, who need additional in-home support. It could even be sacrificing your ego and pride in order to forgive your partner for a wrong done against you. None of these things is *easy*, but this is the fundamental concept behind sacrificial love. We are called to sacrifice something for our partner even when they don't deserve it, because that is what it means to love sacrificially, just like Jesus.

> ***Exploring the Scripture:*** *Read Isaiah 53:5. What feelings come to mind when you read about Jesus's sacrifice for you? Many people only think of Jesus's death when they think of His sacrifice, but Jesus sacrificed more than just His life during His ministry here on earth. What other sacrifices do you think Jesus might have made for you besides His death on the cross?*

Speak Truth in Love

Instead, speaking the truth in love, we will grow to become in every respect the mature body of Him who is the head, that is, Christ.

<small>Ephesians 4:15 (NIV)</small>

D o you think speaking "truth" and speaking in "love" sound like two completely separate things? Like, if I speak the truth, I'm not speaking in love, because the truth hurts, baby. And if I speak in love, I can't speak the truth, because speaking in love means never saying anything that's hard to hear. However, there must be some sort of middle ground in the "truth" and "love" conundrum, because Ephesians 4:15 tells us that when we speak the *truth in love* we will grow to become mature Christians resembling the image of Jesus Christ.

How does this work, especially in the context of a marriage? I can't tell you how many times I've failed to do exactly what this verse tells us to do. I've either spoken truth in a very unloving way, or I've spoken in love but shied away from the truth in an attempt to prevent an argument. However, the goal here is to do *both* at the same time. The reason is that the Bible tells us that without love there is no communication of truth. And the flipside of that is, without the communication of truth, you're not really showing love. The world tells us that the truth hurts, but Jesus tells us that the truth will set us free (John 8:32). Speaking the truth isn't the problem; the problem is the way the truth is being packaged for us to hear.

Let me explain.

Think of your words as if they were a *product* you were trying to sell someone. Most products spend a lot of time in the design phase; but after the product has been perfected, it goes to the marketing department to determine how the product will be packaged. The marketing department is crucial, because sometimes a good marketing technique is what sells the product in the first place. The way a product is packaged *matters.* I have definitely been known to buy one product over the other, *not because it was better*, but because the packaging was prettier. Sad but true.

When it comes to our words, it's no different. In communicating with our partners, the truth in our words should be the *product*, and love should be the *packaging*. So, in order for us to successfully speak truth in love, we need to learn how to become packaging experts.

Here are some examples of bad packaging: a critical tone, acting conceited when speaking to your spouse, rolling your eyes at each other, and cold or impatient body language. Even if what you have to say is true, packaging your words in any of these ways is a surefire way to leave your message undelivered. On the other hand, good packaging includes speaking in a kind tone that's warm and understanding and patiently letting your partner explain their point of view. This type of packaging ensures that what you are saying will not only be heard, but received in a way that can be absorbed and processed.

> **Weekly Opportunity:** *One of the greatest things you can do for your marriage is to learn how to speak truth in love. This skill requires intentionality and practice in order to see improvement, so the best way to improve in this area is to be open with your partner about your efforts. Have a conversation about how you can both improve in speaking truth in love, and ask for feedback on how you can say something in a way that is both truthful and said in love.*

Ultimately, Unforgiveness Only Hurts You

And when ye stand praying, forgive, if ye have ought against any: that your Father also which is in heaven may forgive you your trespasses.

MARK 11:25 (KJV)

Forgiving someone who has wronged you can be one of the hardest things to do. It feels like you're letting that person off the hook scot-free, right? As though what they did to you is okay, and the deep wounds in your heart don't *really* matter. But forgiveness doesn't mean you're okay with the hurt someone has caused you, nor does it automatically erase the pain. God asks you to forgive because He knows that forgiveness is the only pathway *out* of your pain.

I know it sounds counterintuitive, but that's kind of the central theme in the Kingdom of God. God's kingdom is an upside-down kingdom where giving leads to prosperity, loving your enemies leads to greater joy, and forgiving those who hurt you releases *you* from pain.

When you hold onto your anger by refusing to forgive your partner, you actually hold yourself in bondage. You'd think that unforgiveness only causes your partner to suffer, but that's simply not the truth. You are the one who'll be suffering in your own private prison cell, which you built yourself. Do you know what happens to the minds of inmates who spend a lot of time in solitary confinement? Nothing good. Your mind will begin to betray you as you slide down the slippery slope of grief, despair, paranoia, and depression.

This happens because the longer you justify your anger and choose to hold onto those feelings of unforgiveness, the stronger and deeper those feelings of resentment and bitterness will grow. And, although feelings of anger and justification can make you feel in control and satisfied in the moment, these feelings are calling your bluff, because they're endorsed by a false sense of empowerment. The truth is, unforgiveness will *always* hold you back from true happiness and joy, because unforgiveness doesn't lead you down the path of healing and restoration. It leads to isolation and bitterness.

That is why it's crucial not to let even the smallest of offenses take root in your heart. You need to release the pain, and you do that through forgiveness, by asking God to soften your heart and allow you to look upon the person with kindness and love rather than anger and resentment. Forgiving doesn't mean forgetting what they've done; it just means no longer having anger in your heart toward them.

Those who are able to forgive the people who have hurt them the most are also the people who are able to create healthy and fruitful lives and relationships, regardless of the physical or emotional scars they carry. But those who nurse their bitterness and anger remain in the downward spiral of grudge and resentment. It's as simple as that. As the renowned Christian author Lewis B. Smedes once said, "To forgive is to set a prisoner free and discover that the prisoner was you."

I'm not asking you to suddenly become superhuman and not have feelings, but I do want to challenge you to be quick to forgive offenses, because doing so keeps *your heart* clean and free. Remember, forgiveness does not erase the past but instead looks upon it with compassion.

> **Weekly Opportunity:** *It's likely that, as we're talking about forgiveness, something in your heart has begun to stir. So, what I want you to do is close your eyes and picture someone in your life against whom you feel you have been holding a grudge. Share with your partner what that person did to you, and why it's been so hard to forgive them. After each of you shares, pray over each other, asking God to open up your heart and help you forgive.*

Seek God First

But seek ye first the Kingdom of God,
and his righteousness; and all these
things shall be added unto you.

MATTHEW 6:33 (KJV)

The Bible makes it clear that we are called to seek God first, above everything else. When we do that, everything else in life will be given to us, including our marriage. Studies have shown that every human being has four basic needs: acceptance, identity, security, and a sense of purpose. Whom are you depending on to fill them, God or your spouse? It's so easy to bypass God and go straight to the person you can see and touch, but it's a fact of life that all people, *including your partner*, are going to let you down. Maybe not immediately, but it's likely to happen at some point in your marriage. It doesn't mean they don't love you, it just means the person you are marrying is *human*. They are a sinner saved by grace, just like you.

I used to feel completely devastated whenever someone would let me down, because I expected my closest friends and family to be nearly perfect. Then, when I became a Christian, I set the same expectations on my Christian friends, but even more so. I thought, *"These people are Christians*, surely they won't hurt me." Wrong again. And, as you can probably guess, the same expectation of perfection can't be placed on your future spouse, either. Whether you are a follower of Jesus or not, people are just people, and you cannot expect other people to carry your emotional burdens and fill all your human needs.

When you're let down by the people closest to you, it can tear you apart the most. This type of hurt can leave you feeling rejected and heartbroken. That is why we can't lean on other people to satisfy these deep needs. Even the kindest and most loving people can let you down eventually, and if your sense of self-worth is based on how others treat you, then you're in big trouble. That's why Jesus Christ is the only person we can ever truly rely on to meet these needs. Because Jesus was perfect and without sin, He is the only one you can depend on 100 percent, no matter what. Jesus is big enough and capable enough to carry your emotional burdens and meet all four basic human needs.

Now, if your goal is to keep Christ first in your life, you might be wondering what seeking the Kingdom of God first looks like. It's common to hear Christians say, "Make sure you keep God first place in your life," but what does that even mean? Well, simply put, everyone has priorities.

Putting God first means making Him your top priority over everything else. It's not necessarily something you "do" every day; it's how you view God in your heart. Is He your first love above everything else? We arrange our lives and schedules around the things that we *perceive* to be important, so seeking God first means our lives revolve around serving God and living in complete obedience to Him, however that may look to you. It could be through your personal quiet time with the Lord, attending church, prayer, Bible study, or simply fellowshipping with your church community. But here's the truly amazing part: You would think that by doing this you're signing yourselves up for a lifetime of rules, regulations, and general existential suppression, but, in fact, the Bible says that when you lead a Kingdom-first life, every other blessing will be added to you, including a bangin' marriage!

> **Prayer:** *Jesus, help me put you first in all things. Even though I cannot see you or touch you, help me depend on you for my every need. You are my Creator and know me better than I even know myself. Help me seek you and find love, acceptance, and peace through your love.*

Love Never Gives Up

It always protects, always trusts,
always hopes, always perseveres.

1 Corinthians 13:7 (NIV)

Thfis verse is one of the most beloved verses in the entire Bible. My favorite translation is in the English Standard Version (ESV): "Love bears all things, believes all things, hopes all things, endures all things." It's almost lyrical, isn't it? As if it could be a song. The Bible makes it clear that love is the greatest thing in the world, which is why, in 1 Corinthians, Paul wants us to understand love better. To help us understand what love *is*, he breaks down what love *does* into four descriptions: love bears, love believes, love hopes, and love endures. Throughout your marriage you will likely be called to love in these ways, whether through loss of a job, infidelity, death of a parent, trouble with a child, or simply hoping that God will transform the other person's heart. So, let's begin by breaking them down.

To "bear all things" is an antiquated way of saying support and protect, no matter the trial, burden, or annoyance. It doesn't mean we put up with mistreatment or let people walk all over us. What it *does* mean is that, out of genuine passion and concern for another person, love will do everything it can to be respectful regarding the other person's weaknesses and failings. This doesn't mean condoning a harmful or negative behavior (like an addiction or a compulsion). Instead, "bearing all things" means you are more inclined to be discreet when someone does something wrong rather than making sure everybody knows about it. If every time your significant other does something wrong you can't wait to broadcast their faults to your friends, that's not showing them love. True love doesn't expose their partner's wrongdoings but instead is respectful and understanding.

Next, love believes all things. Believing all things means love is not suspicious or cynical. It always believes the best in another person. This is a marker of real love. Again, this doesn't mean ignoring harmful or dangerous behavior but simply viewing your partner without constant accusations and blame. For example, you can tell when someone truly loves you because, in spite of your failures, that person will still see the best in you. If you have an eagerness to believe something bad about another person, that is not love, that's the opposite.

Love hopes all things. This means love is fully optimistic. You never give up on someone but always keep on hoping. However, you're not placing your hope in the actual person but in the Lord. This is the beauty of God's love for us. A person's failures may be great, but they're never final, because the Holy Spirit is *always* in the process of transforming someone into the image of Christ. As long as that person has Jesus in their heart, there is always hope, and where there is hope, there is always love.

Last, love endures all things. In a nutshell, this means you can't kill love, because love always perseveres, through every situation. The word "endures" means to remain firm under suffering or misfortune without yielding. This is huge, because it tells us that true love never gives up. It fights, even to the point of enduring hardship. This tells me we are to fight for our marriages, never giving up on our commitment to God or to each other. A love that endures isn't a love that is easy and without strife; it's a love that, despite hardship and challenges, chooses to persist because of a deep devotion to God and to each other.

> *Exploring the Scripture: Read all of 1 Corinthians 13. You'll find Paul uses many more action words to describe the real meaning of love. Which description of love stands out to you the most? Why do you think that's the case? How can you apply these descriptions of love even more in your life and relationship?*

Two Are Better Than One

---

*Two are better than one; because they
have a good reward for their labour.*

ECCLESIASTES 4:9 (KJV)

Call me crazy, but I kind of love the book of Ecclesiastes. It's known for its depressing and pessimistic demeanor, but I find its truth and accuracy on the meaning of life very refreshing. This book was written by King Solomon, who, it would seem, wrote it during some sort of midlife crisis. It's clear he was frustrated with a lot of things going on around him. One of his observations is an argument he makes in chapter 4 regarding *the advantages of companionship.*

He begins by saying that for a person to be all alone, working tirelessly to gain wealth, is simply meaningless and depressing. (Don't hold back, Solomon, tell us what you really think.) He continues by saying two are better than one because they can help each other succeed. So, Solomon's first point about the benefits of companionship is that it helps *both* parties succeed in life.

Through the inspiration of King Solomon, God is warning us that wanting to do things by yourself, with your own strength, is not wisdom. In a marriage, we will always be more productive as a team. You've heard the quotes—"teamwork makes the dream work," "we rise by lifting others," and "there's no I in team." I could go on, but we'll stop there. Well, chapter 4 of Ecclesiastes actually gives us examples of how this "teamwork" mentality benefits our relationships.

In verse 10, we are told that if one of the two falls down, the one standing can reach out and help. Other translations say the one left standing can lift the other back up. How true is this verse? No matter how independent you are, there will come a point when you'll need the help of another person to lift you back up. This verse isn't talking about someone literally falling down, it's more about the stability we experience when we live life together rather than apart. We need each other to help us up when we stumble and care for us when we're down.

Then, in verse 11, Solomon says that two people sleeping close together will stay warm. Then he asks the reader, how can someone who's alone stay warm? Although there is a practicality behind this verse, (it is warmer when two people are sleeping close together), the verse is really talking about intimacy. Let me ask you this: When you are angry with your partner, do you feel like curling up on the couch and snuggling together? Yeah . . . that's a heck no! When you're angry with your partner, you hardly want them to even look at you, let alone touch you. Your anger creates a coldness in your heart. But when two people are loving and intimate with each other, it's a completely different story. There's a warmth between two people who are intimate because of their mutual level of love and respect for each other. So, as you prepare to join forces, understand that the two of you can do far more together than you could do apart, because of your shared companionship, stability, and intimacy through marriage.

> ***Weekly Opportunity:*** *In what ways are the two of you better together? Each of you write down a list of at least five ways that your lives are better because of your relationship, then compare them.*

Triple-Braided Cord

And if one prevail against him, two shall withstand him; and a threefold cord is not quickly broken.

Ecclesiastes 4:12 (KJV)

You'll often hear this verse quoted at weddings; perhaps it's even being used at yours. In previous verses, Solomon spends a lot of time arguing his case for why two are better than one, which is why it's interesting that he then ends the argument with the idea that three are better than two. In the context of a marriage, you might be thinking, "Solomon, what on earth are you suggesting?" But before you let your mind wander, I'll tell you exactly what Solomon means. When you weave together the lives of a man and woman in holy matrimony, they are stronger together, but they're not strong enough for what life might throw at them. They need a third cord woven into the equation, because a threefold cord is less easily broken. That third cord is the Lord Jesus Christ.

The picture that Solomon presents is that a triple-braided cord is stronger than a single, or even double, stand-alone cord. As the wisdom of Solomon would have it, this is actually sound engineering advice. If you have a single thread and hang a weight on it, it might sustain some weight, but with enough weight added, it will eventually break. The same applies if you have two threads next to each other holding weight. As you add more weight, they will also snap. But, if you keep adding threads to help sustain the weight and then weave those threads together, the braided cord becomes even stronger.

Bridges are actually designed with this concept in mind. If you look at a close-up picture of the Golden Gate Bridge, you'll see that the bridge is actually suspended by a bunch of wires wrapped around each other, forming massive cables. From this we can conclude that when you weave individual cords together, it magnifies the strength of the cord as a unit. However, this verse isn't talking about the engineering of a bridge, it's talking about the weaving together of lives, especially in marriage.

When two people come together in marriage, they will begin to weave their lives together. With just the two cords they can have a good marriage, but to have the *best possible* marriage, they need a third cord. They need Jesus—the third cord that keeps the two together and provides *the most* strength. It's ironic that when a couple gets married, we refer to it as "tying the knot." Well, let's make that knot even stronger by tying it with Jesus at the center. You need to make sure that everything you do has that third cord wrapped around it. That's why a threefold cord is not easily broken. When two people who are committed to serving the Lord come together in marriage, they simply *cannot* lose, because Jesus doesn't *ever* lose. He's undefeated. If you keep Jesus at the center of your relationship, you can't help but succeed.

> ***Weekly Opportunity:*** *How are you making sure you're keeping Jesus at the center of your relationship? Write down 10 ways you can incorporate Jesus into your lives, and each week introduce a new way into your routine.*

Bitter Roots

Looking diligently lest any man fail of the grace of God; lest any root of bitterness springing up trouble you, and thereby many be defiled.

Hebrews 12:15 (KJV)

Even if you don't know exactly what a bitter root is, you can probably guess that it's bad news for your marriage, right? Right. In Hebrew culture, poisonous plants were called "bitter" plants, and because of this the author of the letter to the Hebrews is using a "bitter root" as a metaphor for something that's harmful to the church.

Just as roots are typically only found underground, bitterness is easy to hide. Rarely will you hear someone admit that they are a bitter person. However, the attitude of bitterness can grow and produce fruit of its own kind—and this fruit is poisonous. A bitter person tends to be hypersensitive, sarcastic, pessimistic, ungrateful, insincere, and likely to hold grudges. It can seem harmless because, after all, your bitterness isn't hurting anyone but you, right? Wrong. Hebrews 12:15 says that a bitter root grows up to cause trouble and defile *many*. This means allowing a bitter root to fester doesn't just affect you and your life but can grow to defile those around you. To defile something means to spoil or, more accurately, to pollute.

When you allow a bitter root to grow and fester in your marriage, it's as if you have a bottle of refreshing spring water that you put a drop of poison into. How likely are you to want to drink that bottle of water now? Even if it's just a little drop, the whole bottle is ruined. In the same way, just as one drop of poison defiles an entire bottle of water, allowing a bitter root to fester can destroy your entire marriage. Deuteronomy 29:18 says, "Make sure there is no root among you that produces such bitter poison" (NIV).

There's a reason for such a strong warning—bitterness is a root that grows into division, accusation, and even hatred. We can easily find ourselves in a bitter place, harboring grudges and resentment toward someone, potentially for years! I know of marriages where bitterness has wedged its way so deep into a couple's heart that every time they get in a fight it's like listening to the same old song and dance. It doesn't matter what they are arguing about; somehow the conversation shifts to that one time 10 years ago when he did this or she did that.

This is the bitter root that we are hoping to avoid in your marriage. If you find yourself having repeated arguments around that one thing that never got properly healed and mended, it's very likely that you, my friend, have allowed a bitter root to grow in your heart. The only way to truly uproot this bitterness is to surrender your hurt, anger, and resentment and give it to God. Choose to forgive the person who has hurt you, even if you don't feel like it in the moment, and ask God to heal your heart in the mysterious ways that only He can.

> **Reflection Questions:** *What bitter roots have wedged their way into your relationship? What past hurts and offenses have you never truly discussed or dealt with? As things come to your mind, ask God to help you forgive whoever hurt you and for His healing touch on your heart.*

A House Divided Cannot Stand

And if a house be divided against itself, that house cannot stand.

MARK 3:25 (KJV)

"A house divided against itself cannot stand." That's Abraham Lincoln, right? Well, yes and no. Before it was said by Lincoln, it was said by Jesus Christ (which is exciting—I love when biblical phrases and idioms make their way into modern life). However, the true context behind this verse is not very well known.

Jesus's teaching on the divided house is found in the three synoptic Gospels—Matthew, Mark, and Luke. Because it repeats in all three, we should assume that this story is important for believers to learn, understand, and apply to our lives. In all three Gospels we see Jesus casting demons out of people to the point that even the most disbelieving skeptics can't deny His power and authority. People who were mentally unstable and dangerous are now perfectly rational and content, praising the name of Jesus for their transformation. It is such an evident transformation that even Jesus's most notorious haters, the Pharisees, can't deny these miracles. Because they can't deny Jesus's power, they decide to call into question the *source* of that power. They say that Jesus is only able to cast out demons because He is using the power of Satan.

Jesus responds with a completely logical answer: that a house divided against itself *cannot stand*. Jesus is making the argument that a happy, prosperous, and successful household draws its strength from its unity, not its division. I love the way Matthew 12:26 puts it: "If Satan drives out Satan, he is divided against himself. How then can his kingdom stand?" (NIV). Jesus is essentially saying that it's impossible—and also completely illogical—for Satan to cast himself out. If Satan were to cast demons out of a person, then he is only working against himself by promoting Jesus. It simply doesn't make sense.

In the other Gospels, Jesus uses the example that a *kingdom* divided against itself cannot stand. However, the Gospel of Mark brings this analogy a little closer to home, saying that a *house* divided against itself cannot stand. The New Living Translation (NLT) puts it like this: "Similarly, a family splintered by feuding will fall apart." Jesus is saying that, just as Satan cannot cast himself out without compromising the unity of his kingdom of darkness, two people cannot argue and tear each other down without compromising the unity in their marriage.

In order for a married couple's house to stand strong, their marriage cannot be divided; it needs to be *united*. When a couple begins to disagree and argue without proper compromise and resolution, it tears down their house brick by brick. This isn't to say that you and your partner have to agree on everything (that would be completely unrealistic), but it's how you handle your disagreements that determines whether or not you are divided. If you feel there is division between you and your future spouse, I urge you to do everything you can to deal with it and eliminate it. The strength of any marriage is in proper conflict resolution that creates a foundation of marital *unity*. Remember, God has brought you two together for a reason, and by keeping Jesus at the center of your marriage you can get through whatever comes your way (see "Pray Together, Stay Together," page 108).

> *Reflection Questions: What kind of "house" were you raised in? Was it a divided house where your parents frequently disagreed and argued without proper resolution? Or was it a united house? How has your upbringing shaped your view of marriage? What lessons did you learn? What pitfalls would you like to avoid?*

Let God Direct Your Steps

*The LORD makes firm the steps of
the one who delights in him.*

Psalm 37:23 (NIV)

There are so many uncertainties in life, and as the two of you join together in marriage, you will be faced with battling these uncertainties together as a team. Throughout the course of your marriage, life is bound to throw you a few curveballs where you're not going to know what to do. Perhaps you have an unplanned pregnancy, and the two of you don't feel ready to step into parenthood yet, or perhaps you *are* ready for parenthood, but you struggle with conceiving. The truth is, we don't know what the future has in store for us, but there is someone who does—Jesus. Throughout every season of life, you might experience disappointment and frustration or abundance and blessing. But regardless of where you are on the journey, trust and know that you have a Heavenly Father who will direct your steps if you allow Him.

Psalm 37:23 says the Lord directs the steps of the godly, delighting in every detail of their lives. If you are a believer redeemed by the blood of Jesus, then this verse is for you, my friend. We are never alone in the journey of life. God is always there, directing our path and leading us into the next chapter of our lives. This is amazing, because it means we truly have nothing to fear. Despite the challenges your marriage may face, there is no reason to be without hope. Keep in mind, however, that although it's comforting that God guides our path, at some point in your walk He might take you places you don't want to go.

There may be seasons when you and your spouse will be asked to really press into your faith, believing for a breakthrough in your relationship. Or there may be seasons when you are required to wait for the Lord's perfect timing, which (as I know from experience) always tends to be a tough assignment. This could include waiting for your spouse to receive a promotion at work, or waiting on the Lord for the gift of children.

We must realize that no season of our life is ever wasted, because God uses all of it for our good. When we are in a season of blessing and breakthrough, we are to praise God for His favor upon our lives. And when we are in a season of difficulty and pain, we must realize that there might be something God wants us to gain from this experience. Allow God to direct your steps even in those times of frustration and pain, seeking His will for your life. The Apostle Paul says that these seasons are only temporary afflictions preparing for us an eternal glory that is incomparable (2 Corinthians 4:17).

So, no matter what you face, the good or the bad, take heart in knowing that the Lord delights in every detail of your life. There isn't a single thing He doesn't care about or want to help you with. He delights in you and in your marriage. So, let God direct your steps, trusting that the road He leads you down will be the straightest of paths.

> ***Exploring the Scripture:*** *Read Psalm 32:8, Proverbs 16:9, and Proverbs 3:5-6. What do all of these verses have in common? What assurance do you gain in knowing that God repeatedly says in His word that He will direct our steps?*

Call on Me When You Are in Trouble

And call upon me in the day of trouble: I will deliver thee, and thou shalt glorify me.

PSALM 50:15 (KJV)

D id you know that God doesn't expect you to "make it" on your own? He doesn't expect you to toughen up, put on a good face, and "keep calm and carry on." No, God wants you to *call upon Him* in your times of trouble. He wants you to lay your burdens at His feet and come to Him for rest and restoration. Why? Because your Heavenly Father *cares* about you and wants you to come to Him whenever you are in need. He's not too busy for you; in fact, He delights whenever you call upon His name.

What does it mean to call upon the name of the Lord? Well, it's first mentioned in scripture in Genesis 4:26. Here we see that to "call upon the name of the Lord" means to come together in worship and seek help from God. So, to "call upon the name of the Lord" is to approach Him in thanksgiving and worship, and ask God for help, protection, and guidance.

It's actually the same as God's promise for salvation. God promises in Romans 10:13 that everyone who calls on the name of the Lord will be saved. And just like in God's promise for salvation, He says that when you call upon His name in your day of trouble, He will deliver you. When we call upon the name of the Lord, we recognize that we cannot do life on our own and that we are dependent on Him.

However, the second half of this verse is often overlooked. It essentially says that, after God rescues us, we will "give [Him] glory." Wait a minute. What's all this "glory" business? Well, it's true that God's door is always open to you, but He also wants you to glorify Him and remember what He's done for you. It's so easy to cry out to God in our moment of desperation and then afterward go about our lives, putting God back on the back burner. Does this sound familiar?

I had a friend who was telling me a story similar to this not too long ago. She was going through a really difficult time and was crying out to God for help as if her life depended on it. But then after the season had passed, she forgot about God and went back to business as usual. That's when she told me, "I don't want to be a 'valley Christian' anymore! I only turn to God during the low points of my life or when I need help, but I want to come to God during *every* season of life, not just when I need help."

That's what God wants for us, too. He *wants* to help us, but He also wants us to give Him the glory and remember Him *after* He's rescued us. It's important not only to remember God in the "valleys" of life but to remember and glorify Him in the "mountains" as well.

> ***Reflection Questions:*** *When was the last time you called upon the name of the Lord? What was happening during that time in your life? How did you witness the Lord's help, protection, or guidance in your life? Can you relate to my friend's frustration with being a "valley Christian"? If so, how can you change this in your life?*

Clothed in Love

And over all these virtues put on love, which binds them all together in perfect unity.

<small>COLOSSIANS 3:14 (NIV)</small>

It may be hard to imagine right now, but there may come a point when loving each other becomes something that isn't exactly second nature. Don't get me wrong, to *feel loved* is one of the most beautiful things you can experience, but biblically, love isn't a feeling at all. It's actually an action. In the Bible, more often than not, we see the word "love" used as a verb.

You see, you can *choose* to love someone or not. It's a conscious choice you make on a daily basis. In Colossians 3:14 the writer actually tells us to "put on" love as if it were a piece of clothing. Now, this is interesting, because it means, as easy as it is to "put love on," it's just as easy to "take love off." It's a choice. You can decide to put love on and wear it all day long, or take love off and . . . well, not.

The Bible tells us that "God is love" (1 John 4:8). This is truly remarkable. It doesn't say God has love, shows love, or "puts on" love. This verse is telling us that love is the very essence of *who God is*. God could have revealed His love to us any way He wanted, yet He chose to reveal His love to us through an *action*. Through Jesus's *act* of sacrificial love on the cross, God revealed the depths of His love for us.

Our human understanding of love is usually packaged in words like "spark," "euphoria," "fireworks," or "butterflies." These feelings are great! Although they are beautiful and precious, they're not the be-all and end-all of what love is. True love is something you "put on" even when you don't *feel* like it. True love is loving someone even when they're difficult to love, or when you're not receiving love in return.

Jesus is the ultimate example of this type of love. The very people He sacrificed His life to save rejected Him and hung Him on a cross. Thank goodness the love of God is not just a feeling but an action that can be carried out *despite* how you feel.

So, as you prepare for marriage, remember that you are choosing to love your significant other whether you *feel* like loving them or not. You are making a commitment to put on love, for better or worse, even when this whole "love" thing gets tough.

Weekly Opportunity: How can you "put on" love for your future spouse? Brainstorm some ways you can show love through an action. Maybe you can help run errands when they're stressed or buy them a thoughtful gift just because. Sometimes, simply telling your partner just how much you appreciate them can go a long way. Each of you should create a list of ways you can "put on" love and surprise each other by displaying these acts of love periodically throughout the week.

Pray Together, Stay Together

Confess your faults one to another, and pray one for another, that ye may be healed. The effectual fervent prayer of a righteous man availeth much.

JAMES 5:16 (KJV)

J ames 5:16 is probably one of the most famous Bible verses regarding prayer. However, what I really love about this verse is that it gives us a little sneak peek regarding not only the power of prayer, but how true healing and restoration can come to fruition in our lives. James reminds us here that mutual confession and prayer bring healing, whether that be spiritually, relationally, or even physically. When we get unresolved sin out of the way, it's a way of removing hindrances to the work of the Holy Spirit.

This verse begins with two "action" steps: Confess our faults to one another and pray for one another. James says that the combined result of these actions is that you may get a healing. Sounds good, right? Let's look at action step one, confess your faults to one another. This may be one of the most neglected principles among Christians today. I've found that it's way easier to confess our sins to God than it is to confess our sins to one another. But in a marriage, the openness and vulnerability between the two of you is built in part by being honest with each other, especially regarding the areas in your life where you fall short. Refusing to confess your sins to each other keeps you in secret isolation and is a sign of pride in your life. Read what God says about pride: "Pride goeth before destruction, and an haughty spirit before a fall" (Proverbs 16:18, KJV). If pride ultimately leads to destruction, it makes sense that the path to healing and restoration comes from its opposite, which is the confession of your faults.

So, we are called to confess our sins to God and also to other people, especially our partner whom we may have hurt. So how does this look? It's actually quite simple, if a bit nerve-wracking to live out. It begins with sitting down with your significant other and honestly sharing that you have messed up and sinned against them, and that you need God's forgiveness—and theirs. Confession, plus the second action step—praying for each other—will lead to healing and restoration in your relationship.

Now let's talk about that second step, prayer. We should pray for—and with—each other in all aspects of our relationship. Thank God for each other, pray for each other's protection, pray about your hopes for the future, and pray about troubles you may be having. Pray especially if you are having a fight! Have you ever prayed for someone who had genuinely angered you or wronged you? Well, I have, and I have to say the most bizarre thing happens when you pray for someone who has hurt you: *Your heart begins to get softer.* It's not so much that the situation immediately gets better, but your heart feels better about the hurt. This is the power of prayer, and the reason why the saying "pray together, stay together" is so true. Prayer creates an atmosphere of trust and surrender, where you give the situation over to God so He can intervene and restore all that has been broken (see "Prevention Prayers," page 49).

> **Prayer:** *Father, help us take James 5:16 to heart whenever there is a conflict in our marriage. Help us confess our faults to each other and pray for each other, so our relationship may be healed and restored.*

As for Me and My Family, We Will Serve the Lord

And if it seem evil unto you to serve the LORD, choose you this day whom ye will serve; whether the gods which your fathers served that were on the other side of the flood, or the gods of the Amorites, in whose land ye dwell: but as for me and my house, we will serve the LORD.

Joshua 24:15 (KJV)

D on't you just love this passage? I bet you're already familiar with it, because let's be honest, it's an extremely popular verse. In fact, it's hard to avoid—if you go into any Christian store, you'll find it printed on plaques, Bibles, T-shirts, and towels. You name it, and you can probably find it. The reason this passage is so beloved is because it's an inspirational statement of faith declaring your and your family's commitment to serving the Lord.

These words were said by Joshua, who has one of the greatest stories, and is one of the greatest leaders, in the Bible. Joshua's greatest accomplishment was leading the nomadic nation of Israel into the Promised Land. This is where Joshua 24 picks up. At this point, Joshua has come to the end of his life. He's giving his final statement to the nation before he will retire and eventually die. Joshua begins by summarizing all the amazing things God has done for Israel, how God rescued them out of Egypt and brought them safely into the Promised Land. He concludes with the climatic statement of faith in verse 15: Joshua says that despite everything God has done for Israel, if serving the Lord seems undesirable to them, they need to choose whom they will serve instead. Will they serve other gods, or will they serve the Lord? As for me and my family, he says, we will serve the Lord.

Now, we are faced with exactly this choice on a daily basis. We, too, have the opportunity to look at the world around us and ask ourselves what we want to believe in. Whom do you want to serve? If serving the God of the Bible seems undesirable to you, you have the right to serve any god you want, including yourself. What's interesting is that Joshua doesn't give you the option to serve nothing, because in reality that's not an option. By choosing to not serve the Lord, you *are choosing* to serve something else, whether it be your career, your money, your social status, other relationships, your significant other, or even your family. Joshua says that whether we choose the Lord or not, we are still making a choice. His decision has been made; what about yours?

As you prepare to walk into marriage and begin a family, this choice is yours to make. Whom will you serve? Will you choose to put Jesus first in everything that you do? Now, I don't want you to think that by making this statement of faith you're promising that everything you do will be perfect. Instead, what you are promising is that through everything you do, you will do your best to honor the Lord.

> **Reflection Questions:** *In what ways can you relate to Joshua's declaration of faith? How are the two of you serving the Lord together—in your relationship, home, church, or community?*

Love Is Patient

*Love is patient, love is kind. It does not
envy, it does not boast, it is not proud.*

1 Corinthians 13:4 (NIV)

Allll hearts swoon at the mention of 1 Corinthians 13, because this chapter is otherwise known as the "love chapter." Probably the greatest chapter ever written on love, 1 Corinthians 13 is one of the most popular chapters to be read at wedding ceremonies. However, despite popular opinion, this chapter isn't actually about marital love at all, although it can, and does, encompass that. The chapter is really about love within the body of Christ, otherwise known as the church. The Bible tells us that God is love, and it's because of His great love for us that He has given us the capacity to love. You'll find that love is the key theme of the Bible; Jesus even says in John 13:35 that it's our love for one another that will prove to the world we are His disciples.

That means nonbelievers should be able to pick out a believer from a lineup because of one defining characteristic: the way they love. How well believers live up to that standard is a completely different story, but to love the way we are called to love is certainly an ideal. In the same way, the kind of love described in 1 Corinthians 13 serves as the *highest ideal* for any Christian marriage.

In 1 Corinthians 13 Paul helps us understand what love is by explaining what love *does* and how love *behaves*. Paul does not define love in the abstract by how love feels; he describes love by how it *acts*. And at the top of his list of action words describing love is the statement "love is patient."

Now, when you look at the marriage between Christ and the church, "patience" describes God's love for us perfectly. Even when we were unfaithful or unloving to Jesus, He remained faithful and loving to us. Throughout the Bible, God demonstrates a love for us that is steadfast and consistent, even when we don't deserve it and, in fact, deserve the exact opposite. However, because Jesus's love for us is one of extreme patience, it makes sense for us to also display patient love in our marriages.

So what does Paul mean by "love is patient" in 1 Corinthians 13:4? The Greek word translated as "patient" is *makrothumeo*, which means "extreme patience"—specifically with people, as opposed to patience with a personal pain or negative life experience. It describes a person who is *extremely* slow to anger and virtually never gets angry regardless of how they are being treated—someone who never explodes, retaliates, seeks vengeance, or becomes hostile.

Patience is a very powerful feature of love; however, it's easy to think otherwise and associate patience with weakness. But that couldn't be further from the truth! Think about it: how easy is it to cave in and get annoyed at your future spouse when they've done something you don't like? For me it's extremely easy. That's because retaliation makes you feel good. However, Paul tells us that a Christian who is marked by love carries a tough mandate. We are to patiently love our partners even when they have hurt us, because that is what it means to love others the way Jesus loves you. This means we are not to be quick-tempered with our significant others, but instead love them with patient endurance.

> **Reflection Questions:** *In what ways could you use more patience in your relationship? What areas of your relationship are triggers for you? Ask God to help you with these parts of your life so you can love your future spouse patiently, kindly, and gently.*

Love Is the Greatest

And now these three remain: faith, hope and love. But the greatest of these is love.

1 CORINTHIANS 13:13 (NIV)

If 1 Corinthians 13 is one of the greatest chapters on love (see "Love Is Patient," page 114), verse 13 is one of the greatest verses on love because it lays out the three most powerful forces in the entire universe: faith, hope, and love. As believers, we should dedicate our lives to these three things. We should strive to grow deeper in our faith with Jesus Christ, have hope for the future in everything we do, and have a deep love for God and other people in our hearts. However, out of all of these, *the greatest* is love.

What exactly makes love so great? Well, love is greater than faith and hope, because faith and hope *depend* on love for their existence. Without love, there can be no true faith, because faith without love is empty. As Paul says in 1 Corinthians 13:2, "If I have a faith that can move mountains, but do not have love, I am nothing" (NIV). At the same time, to have hope without love doesn't make sense either, because we hope for the things that we love. The reason we hope is because of the great love in our hearts for the thing we are hoping for. So, love will always surpass faith and hope, because love is the building block of both.

However, 1 Corinthians 13:13 isn't the first time we read that love is the greatest. In Matthew 22:34–40, Jesus teaches that all the Old Testament commandments can be summed up in love—first a love for God and then a love for others. When the Pharisees corner Jesus and ask Him which is the most important commandment in the law of Moses, Jesus says to them, "'Love the Lord your God with all your heart and with all your soul and with all your mind.' This is the first and greatest commandment. And the second is like it: 'Love your neighbor as yourself'" (Matthew 22:37–39, NIV). So, loving God and loving others is the *greatest law* above every other law.

As noted in "Love Is Patient" (page 114), love is the main theme of the Bible. In 1 John 4:8 the Bible even says God is love. So, when you think about it, love is the essence of Christianity. God, who Himself is love, shows us His love through His son Jesus. Then through the love of Jesus, God asks us to pour out love onto others. The concept behind this is that when a person has been transformed by God's love, they will then be so full of His love that they can't help but share it. That is why love is the greatest reality in the life of the church and the dominant characteristic of the body of Christ.

What, then, does this mean for marriage? Marriage is God's analogy for our relationship with Jesus, so it makes sense that everything we do within the context of marriage and beyond should be done with love. Love is the foundation of who we are as believers, and it should be the core of who we are as spouses, parents, and friends. That's why 1 Corinthians 14:1 begins with "pursue love" (ESV). We are commanded to go after love with everything that we have, making it our highest goal.

> **Prayer:** *Lord, help me love like you. Transform me and change my heart so that I can love my partner the way you love me. Your word says that love is the greatest, even above faith and hope, so help me make loving my partner my highest goal.*

The Power of Positive Communication

Death and life are in the power of the tongue:
and they that love it shall eat the fruit thereof.

<small>Proverbs 18:21 (KJV)</small>

Communication is the foundation of every good relationship. When you think back on the beginning of your relationship, I would bet the two of you spent a lot of time just talking. To actually get to know someone, you *have* to spend time with them, and the majority of that time is usually spent talking. However, now that the two of you know each other well (or well enough to commit to marriage), maintaining healthy communication is key for a successful future together.

When reading this verse from Proverbs we should keep in mind that the word *tongue* is often a reference to the spoken word. This means our words have power, and we should be careful with what we say; not all communication is good communication. In fact, poor communication can have devastating effects. The children's rhyme, "sticks and stones may break my bones, but words will never hurt me," is very deceiving. Words can hurt us. And we have to be especially aware that our words can hurt our significant others and our marriages. In fact, the vast majority of marriages end because of reckless verbal mistreatment. Proverbs 12:18 says, "The words of the reckless pierce like swords, but the tongue of the wise brings healing" (NIV).

So when Proverbs 18:21 says there is life and death in the power of the tongue, it means that with your mouth you can either lift someone up or completely tear them down. James 3:6 describes the tongue as "a fire," as if to say, "Who has not been burned by it?" So, if we want to have healthy marriages, we must begin with having healthy communication. When we get into arguments, instead of tearing each other down with our words in an attempt to win, let's understand the power of our words and use them wisely. Kind, supportive speech can bring such strength and healing to a marriage.

This doesn't mean you can never share anything negative in a healthy relationship. Quite the contrary. Healthy relationships require proper communication, even regarding things that are difficult to talk about. The Bible says you are a wise person if you learn to use your words in a proper manner. That means that even if you are saying something that's difficult to hear, you can do it in a way that is still loving and kind (see "Speak

Truth in Love," page 72). Trust me, I know this is easier said than done; there's a reason there are so many proverbs in the Bible on controlling your tongue. Still, the sooner controlling your tongue becomes second nature to you, the better your relationship and marriage will be.

Prayer: *Lord, help me control my tongue in all areas of my life, but especially with my future spouse. Help me only speak words in love.*

Forgiveness Is
Not an Emotion

*Be kind and compassionate to one another, forgiving
each other, just as in Christ God forgave you.*

EPHESIANS 4:32 (NIV)

To some people, forgiveness may seem like weakness, as if you're letting an undeserving person win. But forgiveness has zero connection to weakness or emotions. Forgiveness is a lot like love. It's an act of will. And the will can function regardless of the temperature of the heart.

When you live in a place of unforgiveness, it sparks emotions of hurt, anger, and blame, which tarnish your perception of life. That is why when you do forgive someone, you are letting go of that pain and hatred instead of allowing it to eat at you. Now, I want to make it 100 percent clear that I am with you if you find it difficult to forgive someone who has wronged you. Perhaps that person is even your partner. But regardless of the wrongdoing I want you to consider this perspective: At the end of the day, forgiveness is for your own emotional welfare. It's not just pardoning another person's bad behavior. Forgiveness is really not for the other person's benefit at all—it's for our own (see "Ultimately, Unforgiveness Only Hurts You," page 75).

So, if you're on board the forgiveness train, how do you move past hurts and offenses to a real place of genuine forgiveness, especially when you don't *feel* forgiveness in your heart? Ephesians 4:32 says, "Be ye kind one to another, tenderhearted, forgiving one another, even as God for Christ's sake hath forgiven you" (KJV). When understanding how we can possibly forgive someone who has hurt us so badly, we must remember that Jesus lovingly forgives us for all of the wrongdoing we've done against Him.

Jesus does not forgive us because we've *earned* His forgiveness. (We haven't.) Jesus forgives us because He *loves* us. And because of His great love for us, He asks that we turn to our neighbors who have wronged us and forgive them. We don't forgive because we *feel* like forgiving, or because the person who has hurt us has somehow *earned* our forgiveness. If we waited until those things were true, we might never forgive anyone! Instead, we forgive because God has commanded us to forgive, as dull as that may sound.

Being commanded to do something even when we don't feel like it isn't exactly terrible. Throughout scripture we find a direct correlation between the Lord forgiving us and then our ability to step out in obedience and forgive others. I guarantee there will be times in your marriage when you will feel the prompting of the Holy Spirit to forgive your partner, even if you don't *feel* like it. And when they don't really deserve it. But remember, forgiveness is not an emotion; it's an act of obedience because of the forgiveness you have received from Christ.

> **Prayer:** *Jesus, thank you for forgiving me even when I don't deserve it. Help me forgive others in return, and help me be especially quick to forgive my partner even if I don't feel forgiveness for them in my heart.*

She Laughs without Fear of the Future

She is clothed with strength and dignity;
she can laugh at the days to come.

PROVERBS 31:25 (NIV)

You probably either love or hate these verses about the Proverbs 31 woman. Some women look at Proverbs 31 and feel like it's a burden scripture places on all women to attain some glorious level of wifehood. You can easily call this section of scripture "Superwoman." But women should know that the Proverbs 31 woman is not meant to be an intimidatingly high standard of godly womanhood that you'll forever strive to measure up to. Instead, women (and men) should look at these verses as an elevation of women in general.

Many people think the Bible speaks very poorly of women; however, this passage says otherwise. The Proverbs 31 woman is incredible; her description is actually contrary to what many people assume the Bible says about women. God has created women with wonderful gifts and abilities. His blessing upon women is letting those gifts shine and using them to bless their family and those whom they love.

I want to point out that this iconic description of a woman in Proverbs 31 is actually a poem written by King Lemuel. It's based on the advice his mother gives him regarding how he should behave as king. In the poem, his mother begins by advising him on all kinds of important topics, including the dangers of drinking too much wine and the virtue of standing up for the weak and poor. Then, as any loving mother would do, she advises him on the qualities he should look for when choosing someone to marry. She describes the qualities to be found in a woman of noble character so that when her son meets this woman, he will recognize her.

So, please do not view Proverbs 31 as a to-do list. It is a beautiful, poetic representation of what it means to be a virtuous woman. In fact, in Proverbs 31:30 the author tells us what truly is worth celebrating in a woman: "Charm is deceptive, and beauty is fleeting; but a woman who fears the LORD is to be praised" (NIV). Notice it's *not* the woman with the best job who is to be praised. Nor is it the woman with the most perfect home or car. It's *not* even the woman with a model marriage and well-behaved children. The Bible says a woman *who fears the Lord* is to be praised. A woman who has this type of fear is a woman who is completely in awe of God. She is a woman who honors God by seeking Him in everything she does and trusting Him wholeheartedly with her life.

This woman is clothed in strength and dignity, because she trusts in God with all her heart. She's a woman who draws her strength from the Lord and holds her head high, because she knows her value and worth as a daughter of God. She is not afraid of the future but instead can laugh at the days to come, because she knows that God is always in control and she has nothing to fear.

Exploring the Scripture: Read all of Proverbs 31 together. Challenge yourselves to look at the chapter closely to see which part of this scripture is a gift to you as a couple. Which verses do you still need to learn from? What parts of this scripture inspire you and create in you a desire to be more like this description?

Guard Your Heart

Above all else, guard your heart, for
everything you do flows from it.

PROVERBS 4:23 (NIV)

We don't often think of "guarding your heart" within the context of marriage, because we usually only hear this verse thrown around in church culture when it comes to single-ness. It's treated as a word to the wise for every lonely, single heart—if you want to protect your emotions and feelings and not get hurt in the process of dating, heed Proverbs 4:23 and "guard your heart."

Now, this proverb is a valuable piece of advice no matter your season of life, but it's *especially* applicable when it comes to marriage. The verse doesn't mean you should guard your heart from your future spouse. Instead, you should guard your heart from outside influences that could potentially destroy your marriage. We are to guard our hearts because, as the verse says, everything you do flows from it. Your heart is extremely valuable, and it needs protecting, because your heart is your most authentic self. It's the core of your being. It's where your dreams, desires, and passions live. It's also where you connect with God and share some of the most intimate, private parts of your life with your Creator.

That's why the verse begins with "*above all else*, guard your heart." The author is stressing the importance and seriousness of this proverb. Take note of what this verse *doesn't* begin with. It doesn't say, "when you get around to it," or "if you have the time." Instead, the verse suggests that guarding your heart should be your *top priority*. With that in mind, it's a wonder we don't keep our hearts under lock and key.

Now, let's look at *why* we should guard our hearts. Your heart is the source of everything that you do. Out of the overflow of our hearts we create thoughts, words, and actions. And those thoughts, words, and actions can be positive or negative, depending on the temperature of the heart. A perfect example of this is Jesus's teaching on lust in Matthew 5:27-28. Jesus says, "You have heard that it was said, 'You shall not commit adultery.' But I tell you that anyone who looks at a woman lustfully has already committed adultery with her in his heart" (NIV). This shows us that to Jesus, whether you act on your impulses or simply *desire* them in the deep shadows of your heart, the sin is the same. Even if you've only lusted in your heart, you are still guilty of adultery, because out of your heart comes the action of sin.

So, when it comes to marriage, it is to our *benefit* that we guard our hearts from even the smallest amount of greed, lust, anger, or bitterness. If we don't, these seemingly harmless thoughts done in the privacy of our hearts have the potential to fester and eventually spill over into our words and actions. That is why your marriage needs to be guarded, and it begins with your hearts.

> ***Weekly Opportunity:*** *What are some areas of your life that need to be guarded a bit more tightly? Together make a list of these areas and pray over them, asking God to help you guard these areas of your hearts so they don't grow and fester into words and actions.*

Don't Let the Sun Go Down on Your Anger

Be ye angry, and sin not: let not the sun go down upon your wrath.

EPHESIANS 4:26 (KJV)

L et's talk about anger. I think a lot of people might misguidedly think that to be angry is a sin; however, that's simply not true. Anger is a natural human emotion, and the Bible shows many occasions when even God gets angry. One famous instance is in Numbers 32:13, where God becomes so angry with the Israelites that He makes them wander in the wilderness for 40 years. Then, of course, you have Matthew 21:12-13, where Jesus turns over the tables in the temple when He sees it being used by merchants and money changers.

It's not so much that getting angry is a sin, it's *what we do with that anger* that can lead us into sin. Everyone reacts to anger differently. Some people withdraw and sulk, some yell and slam doors, others throw things and can become violent. We are allowed to be angry, but we need to be aware of where to draw the line regarding how we express that anger.

The idea of not letting the sun go down on your anger implies that we need to deal with our anger immediately, without delay. However, this is not what the verse is saying. Anger is a strong emotion, and it can cloud our judgment and make us say things we don't really mean and will only regret later. The problem is, even words that you don't mean can still have lasting effects on the person who receives them. That's why it's important to not speak in the heat of the moment, but to take a break to collect your thoughts and calm down. If that means waiting a day to talk about whatever it was that made you angry, then so be it.

But now you might be thinking, wait a minute, I thought this verse said to never go to bed angry. Well, let's read it in context with the following verse: "Be ye angry, and sin not: let not the sun go down upon your wrath: neither give place to the devil" (Ephesians 4:26-27, KJV).

Aha! Now we get the true meaning behind the verse. This verse isn't saying that every couple who's having an argument should refuse to go to bed and stay up all night until things have been properly hashed out. That would be silly, wouldn't it? This verse isn't to be taken literally. Instead, what Ephesians 4:26 is trying to tell us is that if you allow a prolonged period of time to go by when you haven't properly dealt with your anger, you risk giving the devil a foothold and allowing bitterness to take root in your heart. Once that happens, you're much worse off than just feeling angry. Now you're letting your anger fester and drive a wedge between you and your partner. So, the next time you get into an argument, take enough time that you can be intentional with your words—so you don't say something you regret—but don't ignore the situation either. Allow enough time to pass so that you can address the problem calmly and in love, and so your anger doesn't turn into a bitter root that can come between you and your spouse (see "Bitter Roots," page 92).

Reflection Questions: When you are upset, do you prefer to talk about the situation immediately, or do you like to wait until you've calmed down to collect your thoughts? Often, couples have a difference of opinion on when an argument should be discussed. Listen to each other's point of view on when you prefer to discuss an argument and why. Then make a plan moving forward for how you will tackle these difficult subjects.

The Hope of Wealth

Charge them that are rich in this world, that they be not highminded, nor trust in uncertain riches, but in the living God, who giveth us richly all things to enjoy.

1 TIMOTHY 6:17 (KJV)

Let's be honest, God has a ton to say in His word about how we should use our money. This is probably one of the hardest things to hear, because *no one* wants *anyone* telling them what to do with their money (myself included). However, finances are one of the biggest reasons for marital strain and divorce, so, as painful as it is, it's probably in our best interests to see what God has to say about how we should be managing our finances. Let's explore what 1 Timothy has to say about this.

At its simplest, 1 Timothy is a letter that Paul is writing to Timothy, who is one of his most trusted and closest companions. Paul shares a lot of wise words with Timothy throughout the letter. So, when we finally arrive at chapter 6, we find that it's the final chapter written, and verse 17 is one of the last sentences in the chapter. Now, here's what's interesting: Immediately preceding 1 Timothy 6:17, it seems like Paul is done with his letter. In 1 Timothy 6:16 we read, "Who only hath immortality, dwelling in the light which no man can approach unto; whom no man hath seen, nor can see: to whom be honour and power everlasting. Amen" (KJV).

I mean, this sounds like Paul's done and signing off, right? Except, he isn't. It's almost as if in an afterthought Paul was like, "Oh yeah, before I go—Timothy, be sure to warn the rich people in the world not to trust too much in their money, because ultimately, it's unreliable. Trust in God instead. Okay, now I'm done. Grace be to you all." Now, I'm making a joke, but this is kind of exactly what Paul is saying. Paul is warning people to not trust in their own finances or possessions, which can come and go, but instead to put their hope in God, who richly provides everything needed for life.

So, the first thing we need to recognize when it comes to money, finances, and financial security is that putting your hope in your wealth is not wise. This probably sounds like the opposite of what you've always been taught—plan for the future, build up your savings, invest in your 401(k), etc. Now, does this verse mean that you *shouldn't* be doing those things? No, not at all. There are plenty of verses throughout the Bible that show God expects us to be good stewards of the money we've been given and make wise financial investments (see "Good Stewards," page 56).

Instead, what Paul is trying to get across is that we shouldn't trust in the security of our finances more than we trust in God. God's ways are not man's ways. Paul knows that putting your hope in money is foolish, because more money cannot give you the perfect marriage and life that it so seductively tells you it can. Don't rely on that shiny silver dollar for marital bliss. Remember to hope only in God, even regarding your finances and the pursuit of wealth.

Exploring the Scripture: Read 1 Timothy 6:10, Hebrews 13:5, and Matthew 6:24. What do all of these verses have in common? What is God trying to tell us regarding how we are to view money? Do you and your partner agree?

Nothing Says "Love" Quite like Forgiveness

Wherefore I say unto thee, Her sins, which are many, are forgiven; for she loved much: but to whom little is forgiven, the same loveth little.

LUKE 7:47 (KJV)

W e've discussed a few different ways you can show love, but honestly, nothing says "love" quite like forgiveness (see "Ultimately, Unforgiveness Only Hurts You," page 75). What I want you to do is to think of forgiveness as a *measurement* of love. My favorite story demonstrating the powerful relationship between forgiveness and love is found in Luke 7:47.

In this passage we see the direct relationship between the measurement of love and the measurement of forgiveness. In this part of the Gospel of Luke, Jesus is over at a Pharisee's house having dinner when an immoral, sinful woman from the city comes to Jesus and begins crying at His feet. She is so overwhelmed with emotion that she begins to wipe her tears away with her hair, kissing his feet and pouring expensive perfume on them.

The Pharisee is disgusted that Jesus would allow such a sinful woman to touch Him; however, Jesus uses this moment to correct that attitude. Jesus explains that the reason she is showing Him so much love is because she has been forgiven of so much sin. A person who has been forgiven of much, loves much. But a person who is forgiven of only a little, shows only a little bit of love.

From this woman we see an overflow of love being poured out upon Jesus because she knew she was sinful, yet Jesus forgave her all the same. The amount a person is willing to forgive indicates the amount that person is willing to love. And Jesus was willing to forgive a lot. You see, Jesus knows that genuine forgiveness is a building block to a genuinely loving relationship. Jesus is willing to forgive every sin you have ever committed because of His great love for you. However, He then asks that you be able to do the same.

I have no doubt in my mind that at some point in your relationship you will be hurt, wronged, or wounded by your partner. But I don't want you to think of this as a sign of marital ruin. Instead, remember that forgiveness is an expression of love and commitment to your partner. In fact, it's because of your great love for each other that you are provided with the capacity for forgiveness.

Think of forgiveness as a manifestation of love. Two people who truly love each other will forgive each other, either because of their empathy and compassion for their partner, or simply out of their obedience to the Lord. Honestly, either works. Two of Jesus's greatest teachings regarding how we are to treat each other are to love each other and to forgive each other. The same people we are called to love are the same people we are called to forgive. Which—spoiler alert—is everybody, not just your partner. As Christians we don't get to pick and choose whom we forgive. We are called to show love and forgiveness to everyone, beginning with the people closest to you, especially your partner.

> **Reflection Questions:** *Read Luke 7:36-50, the story of Jesus being anointed by the woman who has sinned. What does this story teach you about the correlation between love and forgiveness? Whom can you relate to more, the Pharisee or the sinful woman? How does this story touch your own life when it comes to Jesus's love and forgiveness for you?*

Money and Marriage

For which of you, intending to build a tower, sitteth not down first, and counteth the cost, whether he have sufficient to finish it?

LUKE 14:28 (KJV)

W ho's never heard that money problems are the leading cause of divorce? We tend to believe that money is the most serious issue in marriage, but is it really? I once overheard a conversation where, when someone brought up the idea that money was the primary reason for divorce, a divorced man shook his head and said, "No. People don't get divorced over money. They get divorced over what money brings out in them."

True or false? I'm going to have to go with true.

But let's not be blind to the fact that money can be a real cause for strife. I would argue that it's not so much that money arguments are more hurtful or more divisive than other arguments, it's simply that money is literally *everywhere*, and so are decisions regarding money. It's unavoidable!

We make decisions regarding money every single day. Will I pack my lunch today or eat out? I ran out of shampoo; should I get more deodorant and toothpaste while at the store? I haven't splurged in a while; should I finally get that new dress I've been eyeing? Every single day we are consciously or unconsciously calculating whether various items are "worth" buying or not. And to top it all off, buying things is sometimes more of an emotional decision than a practical one, because when you buy something, it also affects the way you *feel*. So, in that way, spending money can be a trigger for positive self-esteem and emotional well-being.

And with all of these financial decisions reverberating at low frequencies throughout every single day of our lives, it's no wonder that money can become a problem in marriages. I mean, all of these daily financial decisions are hard enough to manage by yourself, but throw another person in the mix, and it can feel like complete chaos. Especially if the person you are saying "I do" with has a completely different perspective on how to manage money.

Without a doubt, money can create a relational strain. But any couple who has survived financial heartache will say that if you have a close relationship, you can overcome anything—financially speaking or otherwise. Is there a formula for marital bliss regarding finances? Well, I think Luke 14:28 is a good starting place.

What I want you to do is think of your married life as if you were building a tower. There are many expenses that go into building a tower, just like when you first get married there are many expenses that go into establishing a life together. Too often, couples put off financial planning until they are so deeply in debt that trying to get out of debt feels nearly impossible. However, that's not financial planning, that's financial *reacting*. What Luke 14:28 is saying is that in order to build for the future, you need to sit down and count the cost *ahead of time*, not after you're up to your ears in bills. This means a budget and proper financial planning are key to a successful marriage (see "First Fruits," page 62).

> **Weekly Opportunity:** *You're probably being faced with all kinds of expenses at the moment, like a wedding, a honeymoon, a home, and home furnishings, not to mention any previous student loan or consumer debt. What I am suggesting is (the most dreaded of all words), sitting down together and scratching out a* budget *for your marriage. Once you are both able to take an honest look at your income and expenses, then you can properly plan for your future with a budget that works the best for you.*

You Lose Your Life to Find It

For whosoever will save his life shall lose it;
but whosoever shall lose his life for my sake
and the gospel's, the same shall save it.

MARK 8:35 (KJV)

Thing is verse is one of the most complicated verses in the Bible, but I have to be honest, it's also one of my personal favorites because *it's just so perplexing*. It truly shows us how the rules of God's kingdom are flipped upside down and directly oppose the rules of the world. Mark 8:35 is a perfect example of this. It says that whoever wants to save their life will lose it, and whoever loses their life for Jesus's sake will find it. This verse is one of those Jesus head-scratchers where, all of a sudden, it's like everything you thought you knew to be true about the world no longer is. In Jesus's world, 1+2 no longer equals 3 but could equal 10. The rules of His kingdom are different from the rules of the world, and as believers we'll be spending the rest of our lives figuring out how to do the math.

What Jesus means in Mark 8:35 is a little biblical concept that the Christian world calls *dying to self*. Dying to self is part of being born again, except it's not a onetime event but a *lifelong process*. Jesus repeatedly tells His disciples that if they are truly His followers, they are to take up their cross (a symbol of death) and follow Him. Jesus never sugarcoats the Christian walk. Instead, He makes it painfully clear that if *anyone* wants to follow Him, they must deny themselves and surrender everything for the sake of the gospel, including their wants, their desires, and even their lives. Jesus says that if you try to save your earthly life, you will lose your life in the Kingdom of God. But if you are willing to sacrifice your earthly life for Jesus's sake, then you will find eternal life in the Kingdom of God.

Now, these very powerful and strong words coming from Jesus truly make you rethink the Christian walk. It's a walk of self-sacrifice and self-denial, which isn't exactly easy. However, I think this exact same concept can easily be applied within the context of marriage. Whoever comes into their marriage trying to save their own life will lose their marriage. But whoever comes into it willing to lose their life for Christ's sake, and for the sake of the marriage, will save it. Meaning, if you only value your marriage for the ways it can serve you and your needs, then you will lose your marriage. But if you come to your marriage with the intention of serving your spouse and their needs, then you will save your marriage (see "True Love Is Sacrificial," page 69).

For example, at some point in your marriage your spouse could become ill, and you may need to nurse them through that illness. Or perhaps your partner will want to pursue their dream job, but that would require a relocation that is less than ideal for you. These acts of self-sacrifice for the benefit of your partner might be difficult to do, but this is how we show them true love. We find throughout the Bible that self-sacrifice is the epitome of the Christian walk, and I would contend that it's also the formula for a healthy Christian marriage. It is only when we selflessly love our partners in patience and kindness that we see our marriage absolutely flourish (see "Submit Yourselves to Christ," page 40).

> **Reflection Questions:** In what ways have you "died to self" throughout your Christian walk? What benefits have you reaped from walking in the ways of the Lord? When it comes to loving your partner, in what ways could you love them more selflessly?

Train a Child in the Way He Should Go

Train up a child in the way he should go: and when he is old, he will not depart from it.

Proverbs 22:6 (KJV)

"Train up a child in the way he should go: and when he is old, he will not depart from it" is probably one of the most famous parenting verses ever quoted. A lot of people know this verse like the back of their hand and cling to it whenever they're faced with an unruly child who, later in life, has decided to depart from the Christian faith. Now, if this is you (or if you know someone to whom this applies), I apologize, but this verse is actually not all that it appears to be. This verse is actually up there for being one of the most *mistranslated verses* in the Bible.

Today this verse tends to get used as a promise from God to encourage parents with wayward children. People who use the verse in this way hold out hope that because they raised their child in the church, someday they will repent and come back to Christ. It can also be used with a negative connotation, as if to blame parents whose kids aren't serving God as perhaps they wish they would. People who use the verse in this way hold the belief that if the parents had raised their children better in the church, they would be more devoted Christ-followers.

Now, the reason these interpretations are incorrect is because many people misunderstand the very definition of what a proverb is. A proverb is not a promise; a proverb by definition is a general truth or wise advice. Proverbs actually create their own category of literature that is found not only in scripture but in just about every other culture as well. However, when it comes to the proverbs found in the Bible, many readers misunderstand what a proverb is, assuming proverbs can be applied to their lives as promises from God. That is why the verses found in the book of Proverbs are typically taken as wholesale promises, when in fact, that was never the author's intention. Does this mean the wise statements found in the book of Proverbs aren't true? Not at all. They're still *very true*, but you have to understand what you're reading. Proverbs are not to be thought of as a foolproof guarantee but as wise advice and general truth.

So, what does this mean for those of you who intend to have children and were depending on Proverbs 22:6 as a surefire way to securing your child's future salvation? Well, although there are always exceptions, Christian parents have a tremendous ability to impact their kid's belief system by raising them in the way of salvation through Jesus Christ. This doesn't mean forcing them into a certain set of beliefs, but rather leading them through example by living out your own faith. Of course, all children have free will and the potential to depart from that way, but as Proverbs 22:6 tells us, children who are raised with a reverent fear of the Lord are likely to stay on the right path.

> *Weekly Opportunity: It's important to have a discussion ahead of time regarding how you would like to raise your children. Is raising them in the Christian faith something you both agree on? If so, brainstorm a list of things you can do with your children to teach them these principles. This can include going to church regularly, praying before meals and bed, and even family Bible studies.*

Cast Your Cares
on the Lord

Casting all your care upon him; for he careth for you.

1 PETER 5:7 (KJV)

This verse is literally everything to me. Why, you might ask? Because the peace of mind that comes from knowing that God can handle my stress, anxiety, struggles, and doubts is simply heaven. There are so many things in life that overwhelm me, but to know that I can place my burdens and anxiety on God (and not have to tackle any of them alone) gives me so much confidence and assurance. Not confidence in myself but in God. Whatever comes my way, I know that God is big enough to handle it. By casting our cares on the Lord, we're relinquishing control and saying, "God, I can't even begin to fix this, but you can. I don't know how you're going to do it, but I know that you can see me through."

One of my favorite songs is "Cast My Cares" by Finding Favour. This song, which calls Jesus "the anchor of my hope," came to me in the midst of an especially difficult season. As I was listening to the lyrics, I could feel my anxiety melting away. The idea that God could carry my burdens was a stress reliever in-and-of itself. There is a peace and comfort in knowing that you're not alone in the world. We serve a God who is good, who is sovereign, and who is in complete control of not only your life but everyone else's. And to top it off, He *promises* to work all things for the good of those who love Him and are called according to His purpose (Romans 8:28). This is good news, my friend!

However, you might be wondering, *exactly what does it mean to cast your anxiety on God?* Well, in the Bible, "casting" is when someone or something physically *carries* something for you. They are lifting your load. In the same way, when you cast your burdens onto God, He is lifting the load that's making you feel weary and weighed down. He is literally carrying your burdens for you.

Now you might be wondering, yes, but how *exactly* do I cast my cares on God? Well, you do it by *trusting* Him. You begin by trusting in the fact that God cares for you and that He will never leave you or forsake you. At the times you need Him the most, He will *always* be there for you. Casting your cares onto God actually goes hand in hand with humbling yourself, surrendering your situation to God, and asking Him for help.

It's realizing that God is God and you are not, and understanding that although your abilities may be limited, God's abilities are not.

There may be times throughout your marriage when your partner could be laid off from their job, leaving you to financially support the family. In times like these, we must trust that all is not lost. These are the exact moments when we are to cast our cares onto God and trust in Him for provision, comfort, and help. So no matter what your marriage may go through, nothing is too big or too difficult for God. Cast your cares onto Him, because He cares deeply for you.

> **Weekly Opportunity:** *Listen to the song "Cast My Cares" by Finding Favour. How does this song help you understand 1 Peter 5:7? How does knowing these things give you peace?*

Do Everything in Love

Do everything in love.

1 CORINTHIANS 16:14 (NIV)

I want to share with you a common situation I see between couples. At some point there may be a communication breakdown in your relationship where you think you are showing your partner love, but they aren't receiving it as love at all. Even though you are trying your best to show love to your partner, it's very possible they might still feel *unloved.* I am warning you now, this will be very frustrating for both of you.

Not too long ago I was talking to a friend of mine about this very problem. Her husband claimed he was trying his best to make her feel loved, yet she complained that she didn't feel loved by him at all. To her it felt as if there was this gaping canyon between the two of them emotionally, and they just didn't know how to bridge the gap. After discussing the situation with her to exhaustion, I threw my hands in the air and finally said, "Why don't you just tell him *exactly* what he can do that will make you feel loved." She seemed annoyed and said, "I will never do that. If he really loved me, he would already know what to do."

Okay, now we were finally getting somewhere! I could finally zero in on the problem. *My friend and her husband were speaking different love languages.* Her assumption was that if her husband truly loved her, he would automatically know *the best way* to love her. But that simply wasn't true; he was trying to show her love, but his efforts were getting lost in translation. Devoted partners can sometimes become frustrated lovers because the way they are *offering* love is not always the same way their partner wants to *receive* love. And when our "love communication" isn't being properly received, it leaves our partner feeling unloved, when in reality they may be loved very much.

So how do we fix this problem? Well, one of the greatest books ever written on this subject is called *The 5 Love Languages* by Gary Chapman. I highly recommend you read it, but the basic premise of the book is that there are five main languages people use to give and receive love: words of affirmation, acts of service, gifts, quality time, and physical touch. If you gravitate toward one or two specific love languages, you will tend to show love to your partner in that way and also want to receive love in that way. Let's take a look at each of them.

If words of affirmation are your partner's love language, they value a verbal or written expression of love and appreciation. In this case, thoughts like *"they should know how much I love them, so I shouldn't have to say it"* will never fly.

Acts of service are for the people who feel like actions will always speak *louder* than words. They tend to appreciate love shown through actions—taking out the trash, cleaning up the dishes, or vacuuming the house.

The language of gifts can easily be misunderstood as materialistic, but it's often more about the sentiment and thought behind the gift than the gift itself. It can be as simple as grabbing your partner their favorite snack when you're at the store. It expresses to your partner that they are on your mind.

Quality time is probably the easiest love language to understand, but make no mistake, it's still tricky. It's not so much that your partner needs the two of you to spend more time together, but it's more about the *quality* of the time spent. What your partner truly desires is your attention. That means they need you to listen carefully and respond with thoughtful feedback and not be distracted by social media or the game playing in the background. Basically, you need to be mentally present.

Last, we have physical touch, and before you get too excited—no, we're not only talking about sex, although that is very likely a big part of it. For the person whose love language is physical touch, holding hands, cuddling, kissing, and hugging are how your partner will feel the most loved by you.

Taking the time to understand your partner's love language, and then showing them love in their love language, will take you far in your marriage. As Christians, we know that showing love to others is one of God's greatest commandments, so loving your partner to the fullest should be your highest goal in living out that commandment.

Weekly Opportunity: Now it's your turn! As you were reading, I bet you were already trying to determine what your love language is. But guess what, you don't have to guess. Go online and take the free 5 Love Languages Quiz to discover your own unique love language right now. Share your results with your partner. Were you surprised by your results? Were you surprised by your partner's results? Make a list of ways you can show your partner love by using the love language they receive the best.

The Edge of Burning

That the trial of your faith, being much more precious than of gold that perisheth, though it be tried with fire, might be found unto praise and honour and glory at the appearing of Jesus Christ.

1 PETER 1:7 (KJV)

D id you know that marriage is one of the most effective tools to help us be more like Jesus? We get married and think, "Well, this is going to be a piece of cake. I can't image why people struggle in marriage." Then it doesn't take long to realize *exactly* why people struggle in marriage, because you begin to struggle, too! Then you start thinking, "How on earth does anyone actually *stay* married?" And it's at precisely that point when (if you let Him) God begins to work on your heart and changes you, little by little, making you more like Jesus. Marriage is a beautiful thing. Though there will be good times and bad, it is the bad times that refine you into a more Christ-like person. It is through this refining process that God is actually using your marriage to stretch and sharpen you for heaven. The Bible refers to it as the trial by fire or the furnace of affliction, but I like to call it *the edge of burning*.

I like to use this term within the context of marriage because the romantic relationship, especially in the early stages, is white-hot with fire and passion. But fast-forward a few years, and you may find yourselves having moments when you burn against each other in anger and spite. However, that's precisely when God enters. Even though there may be rough patches in your marriage, you'll find that when you lean on God through those rough times, the outcome will be a polishing and smoothing of your marriage, rather than complete destruction. And the longer you two are married, the smoother and more polished you will become. Thus, the more like Jesus you will become! That is God's intention and purpose for marriage. It's not just about always feeling happy, raising kids, or having the picture-perfect family at church. It's a process where you allow marriage to *refine* you into a person who is more loving, patient, humble, kind, and ultimately, more like Christ.

In 1 Peter 1:7 we read that various trials *are proof* of the genuineness of your faith, which is more precious than gold. This is because perseverance *proves* your faith. So, when your faith remains strong even when it is tested by fire, it will bring God much glory, praise, and honor. As much as we hate to suffer, it is in the hard times that we grow the most, because *trials develop godly character*. So, when you find yourself losing patience or getting frustrated with your partner, remember that this is an opportunity for God to sharpen and refine you through the testing of fire. God doesn't want you and your partner to suffer in your marriage, but He will surely use it to mold and shape you for His purposes and ultimately for your good.

> ***Reflection Questions:*** *As God refines you through the fires of marriage, you will be stretched and sharpened into a person who sacrifices, serves, and loves like Christ. How has God already refined you through your walk with God? In what ways has your life, and the lives of those around you, been blessed from that refining process? What areas of your life do you already know you could improve in?*

Grace, Mercy, and Peace

Grace be with you, mercy, and peace, from God the Father, and from the Lord Jesus Christ, the Son of the Father, in truth and love.

2 JOHN 1:3 (KJV)

I find that the words "grace" and "mercy" are often used interchangeably, but they actually do not mean the same thing. They are inherently related, which is most likely why people confuse the two. If it helps, you can think of them as two sides of the same coin when it comes to salvation, because when God saves a person, He extends both mercy and grace. *Mercy* is forgiving the sinner and withholding the punishment that is justly deserved. *Grace* is when God then extends undeserved blessings upon that person; it's the concept of undeserved kindness, the free and unmerited favor of God. But my personal favorite definition for God's grace is God giving us what we don't deserve. We deserved the punishment of hell, but God graciously bestowed on us the gift of His Son.

Still confused? Here's an example. Let's say you're walking down the street and suddenly realize that someone's trying to pickpocket you. You catch them in the act, and they immediately apologize, explaining the state of desperation that brought them to stealing in the first place. Mercy would be pardoning their actions and not calling the police or pressing charges. However, if on top of that you decided to give them some money to help them out—*that's grace*. See the difference? Mercy is withholding deserved punishment, and grace is bestowing a blessing on top of it, showing undeserved kindness. And the craziest part of this whole story is, *this is exactly how God treats us!* Despite our constant sin and rebellion (even after being saved), God continues to pardon our sins and shower us with every heavenly blessing and gift instead. It's mind-boggling. And as you probably guessed, because Jesus is always our example for how to live, this is how we are to treat others.

So, when it comes to showing grace and mercy in relationships, mercy would be not behaving negatively toward your partner, even if you feel they deserve it. Grace would be going out of your way to show compassion and love toward them, even if you think they might not appreciate it or return the kindness. Sound like a tall order? That's okay—for the believer trying to live this out, the motivation for showing grace and mercy always comes from the grace-giver Himself, Jesus Christ.

God gives us His grace, mercy, and peace, so that we can give them to others. It's by drawing close to Jesus that we are able to show kindness and love toward our partners the way Jesus would want us to. I find that when we are showing our partners grace and mercy, peace always follows—peace in your relationship, peace in your family, and peace in your mind and soul. God promises us that if we ask, it will be given to us (Matthew 7:7). So, as you prepare to enter into marriage, ask for an overflow of His grace, mercy, and peace.

> **Prayer:** *Heavenly Father, thank you so much for bestowing upon us your grace, mercy, and peace. As we enter into marriage, we ask for a double portion of every heavenly blessing you can give us. Help us show each other grace and mercy in our marriage, and help this lead us toward a lifetime of love and peace.*

God Has Plans for Your Marriage

"For I know the plans I have for you," declares the LORD, "plans to prosper you and not to harm you, plans to give you hope and a future."

JEREMIAH 29:11 (NIV)

A common theme I hear from Christian singles is how they are constantly praying for their future spouses. They pray that God will strengthen their future partner to be a mighty man or woman of God, and that in God's perfect timing He will bring that special person into their life. However, it seems that when they find the person God has for them, that prayer warrior mentality slowly begins to fade. It's like we think that God's work is done when He brings us our partner, but the truth is it's only just beginning. There are great and mighty things God wants to do in and through your relationship, and you need to keep praying and pressing into exactly what that is.

Jeremiah 29:11 tells us that God knows the plans He has for you, and these plans are to prosper you and give you a future and a hope. This verse is extremely hopeful, but within its original context we find that it is said only after a bleak turn of events for the Israelites. You see, as a punishment for the sins of Judah, God sends the Babylonians to destroy Jerusalem and the temple and to carry away the people of Judah, forcing them to live in exile in Babylon. At the time of Jeremiah 29, some Jews have already been exiled; however, the destruction of Jerusalem and the temple haven't happened yet. Jeremiah writes to the exiles in Babylon promising them that God has not forsaken them and that they will return to their land one day. He tells them that God has plans for them and their future, and that their nation will be restored. The fulfillment of these plans will be God's son Jesus, a Jew, saving all the nations of the world.

So, you might be wondering, how does this story apply to you, your life, and your future marriage? Is it fair to take the promise God bestowed upon the Israelites and claim it for yourself? Well, yes, most definitely. The reason is because this verse reflects the general nature of God's grace and affection for those He loves, which by the way, is you! So, you can 100 percent apply this verse to your life, because God's nature is unchanging; He remains the same yesterday, today, and forevermore. What God promised the Israelites over 2,000 years ago is also promised to *you*, because God has plans for those who are in Christ, and His plans are always for good.

Make no mistake, Jesus gives us zero expectation that believers in Him will be spared from hardship and persecution. However, He does promise that through that hardship, He will never abandon us. There is overwhelming victory for all who are in Christ Jesus (Romans 8:37). I don't want to leave you with the expectation that as a believer in Christ you will have a marriage that will be perfect and without hardship, but I do want to leave you with the hope that, through it all, God will be with you. If you will allow Him, God can do great and mighty things in and through your marriage that give you, your family, and those around you a future and a hope.

> *Weekly Opportunity: Spend some time with the Lord today asking Him what special calling He has for your future marriage. What about the two of you being joined together in marriage will expand the Kingdom of God? There is a purpose and a mission for every godly marriage. Spend some time in prayer pressing into yours.*

Resources

Chapman, Gary. *The 5 Love Languages: The Secret to Love that Lasts*. Chicago: Northfield, 1992.

Eggerichs, Emerson. *Love and Respect: The Love She Most Desires, the Respect He Desperately Needs*. Nashville, TN: W Publishing Group, 2004.

Farrel, Bill, and Pam Farrel. *Men are Like Waffles, Women are Like Spaghetti: Understanding and Delighting in Your Differences*. Eugene, OR: Harvest House, 2001.

Keller, Timothy, and Kathy Keller. *The Meaning of Marriage: Facing the Complexities of Commitment with the Wisdom of God*. New York: Dutton, 2011.

Kendrick, Stephen, and Alex Kendrick. *The Love Dare*. With Lawrence Kimbrough. Albany, GA: Sherwood Baptist Church, 2008.

Omartian, Stormie. *The Power of a Praying Husband*. Eugene, OR: Harvest House, 2001.

Omartian, Stormie. *The Power of a Praying Wife*. Eugene, OR: Harvest House, 1997.

Thomas, Gary. *Sacred Marriage: What If God Designed Marriage to Make Us Holy More Than to Make Us Happy?* Grand Rapids, MI: Zondervan, 2000.

References

The 5 Love Languages. "Learn Your Love Language." Accessed January 2, 2021. 5LoveLanguages.com/quizzes.

Bahr, Stephen J. "Social Science Research on Family Dissolution: What It Shows and How It Might Be of Interest to Family Law Reformers." March 2, 2001. Presented at the conference, "The ALI Family Dissolution Principles: Blueprint to Strengthen or to Deconstruct American Families?," J. Reuben Clark Law School, Brigham Young University, Provo, UT, February 1, 2001. Fact.on.ca/Info/divorce/bahr2001.pdf.

Barna. "Born Again Christians Just as Likely to Divorce as Are Non-Christians." September 8, 2004. Barna.com/research/born-again-christians-just-as-likely-to-divorce-as-are-non-christians.

Feldhahn, Shaunti. "Busting Cultural Myths about Marriage and Divorce." May 29, 2014. Shaunti.com/2014/05/busting-cultural-myths-marriage-divorce.

Harvey, Philip D. "Divorce for the Best." *Washington Post,* July 11, 2000. WashingtonPost.com/archive/opinions/2000/07/11/divorce-for-the-best/91fad55e-5fa7-4ef0-82c4-2fff7e68e13c.

Smedes, Lewis B. *Forgive and Forget: Healing the Hurts We Don't Deserve.* San Francisco: HarperOne, 1996.

Spurgeon, Charles Haddon. "The Sheep before the Shearers." *Metropolitan Tabernacle Pulpit*, vol. 26. January 1, 1970. Spurgeon.org/resource-library/sermons/the-sheep-before-the-shearers/#flipbook.

Acknowledgments

Whenever something of value is created there are endless people to thank for their inspiration, encouragement, and wisdom. This book is no different. I could not have written this devotional without the efforts of those who have also tackled the topic of love and relationships from a Christian perspective. Thank you all. You have changed my mindset and the mindset of millions with your dedication done in pure service for the Kingdom of God.

I want to start by thanking Pastor Paul LeBoutillier of Calvary Chapel, Ontario, OR, Pastor Skip Heitzig of Calvary Church, Albuquerque, NM, and Pastor David Rosales of Calvary Chapel, Chino Valley, CA. You have each transformed my walk with the Lord in ways you'll never fully know. A simple "thank you" just doesn't seem to cut it; I am forever grateful to each of you.

Thank you to Charity Harang and Isabel Lagos for always being there for me. Thank you to my family for your love and support, and thank you to everyone who has shared stories with me, proving the Lord will never fail you when you submit your love life to Him.

Last, thank you to my Lord and Savior Jesus Christ, who saw me when no one else did and believed in me when I didn't even believe in myself. My life was forever changed when you called me to follow you.

About the Author

 **Tiffany Nicole** is the writer and founder behind the popular Christian blog *Lavender Vines* and the Christian greeting card business by the same name, Lavender Vines Co. Tiffany currently resides in San Diego, California, where she enjoys writing from local coffee shops and spending time with her church community.

Visit the author at LavenderVines.com and on Instagram at @XoTiffanyNicole.

CPSIA information can be obtained
at www.ICGtesting.com
Printed in the USA
JSHW020139020521
14193JS00001B/2